Marietta Marcus

JUNG AND SEARLES

JUNG AND SEARLES

A comparative study

David Sedgwick

London and New York

First published 1993
by Routledge
11 New Fetter Lane, London EC4P 4EE

Simultaneously published in the USA and Canada
by Routledge
29 West 35th Street, New York, NY 10001

Typeset in 10/12 pt Palatino by
NWL Editorial Services, Langport, Somerset

Printed and bound in Great Britain by
Biddles Ltd, Guildford and King's Lynn

British Library Cataloguing in Publication Data
A catalogue record for this book is available from the British Library.

Library of Congress Cataloging in Publication Data
Sedgwick, David, 1951–
Jung and Searles: a comparative study / David Sedgwick.
p. cm.
Includes bibliographical references and index.
1. Psychoanalysis. 2. Jung, C.G. (Carl Gustav), 1875–1961.
3. Searles, Harold F. (Harold Frederic), 1918–
4. Psychotherapy. I. Title.
BF173.S442 1993   93–3266
150.19'54 – dc20   CIP

ISBN 0–415–09698–7

To Chris (July 4, 1983)

'Now is the winter of our discontent made glorious summer . . .'

CONTENTS

CONTENTS

FOREWORD

The aim of this book is to create a relatively unified theory of psychotherapy out of the ideas of C.G. Jung and Harold Searles, two psychologists whose writings have meant a great deal to me personally. Before writing the original manuscript in 1983, I had carefully studied and worked with Jung's theories for almost ten years and Searles' for about five. The study's intensive as well as personal dimensions therefore made it a fitting conclusion to my doctoral training.

Revising it ten years later, I found to my surprise that little had changed in the basic conceptions outlined. Certain understandings had deepened since the original writing, while increased clinical and personal experience had filled in the gaps and rounded off some edges. The model had proved it could float, for me at least – a reliable boat.

In an important sense this book is not only a comparative study of the works of Jung and Searles. Again, it is also an attempt to synthesize their two theories into a third and somewhat new thing. Harold Searles did not particularly like this integration in fact, at least not in its earlier, dissertation form. He felt it denigrated his own, original research contributions. I do not know how Jung would have felt. Whether the synthesis is successful or useful, whether it is fair to its subjects or not – I leave such questions to the reader to decide.

Except for the first chapter, which is a statement of purpose, the core chapters of this detailed study are each followed by a summary for quick review. Each chapter outlines and compares ways that Jung and Searles think (or Jung–Searles together might think) about its topic. The chapter on psychopathology is about how they think about patients, the next chapter reflects their views on the therapeutic process (which means patients and therapists together), and the next one reflects their ideas about therapists. There is an effort to draw all this together at the end.

David Sedgwick, PhD
Charlottesville, VA

ACKNOWLEDGMENTS

Before this book was a book, it was a doctoral dissertation. The specific suggestion to write about Jung and Searles originally came from my wife, Sher Nilson Sedgwick. To her I express my gratitude, both for the idea and for her support in ways too numerous to mention and too deep, really, to give words to.

Tom Fiester, Jim Downton and Phyllis Kenevan, all of the University of Colorado, also directly or indirectly encouraged me to write a thesis about what mattered to me. Many years later several analyst-members of the Library of Analytical Psychology Editorial Committee offered helpful comments on the text, which I utilized.

My very special thanks to Andrew Samuels, who was 'midwife' (as he aptly put it) to the manuscript. He graciously and patiently guided the manuscript into the hands of interested parties, including David Stonestreet of Routledge.

Acknowledgments are due to Princeton University Press for permission to quote from Volume 16 of *The Collected Works of C.G. Jung*; also to International Universities Press for permission to quote from Harold Searles' *Collected Papers on Schizophrenia and Related Subjects* and *Countertransference and Related Subjects*.

1

INTRODUCTION

> I have succeeded in establishing pleasant working relations
> with my one-time opponents, some of the leading minds
> among the Freudians here.
>
> (Jung, 1945)

In the last decade Jungian analysts have become increasingly
interested in the work of the American psychoanalyst Harold
Searles. This is in keeping with Jungian attempts in general to
integrate other psychoanalytic theories. The foremost of such
efforts has been by Jungian analysts in London's Society of
Analytical Psychology (SAP), who have successfully assimilated
the theories of Klein, Winnicott, Racker, Bion and others. The
SAP's work over four decades has remedied particular deficits in
Jungian developmental theory and in analytic technique. While
their syntheses have created some controversy, that controversy
has been dynamic and, usually, creative. In addition, recent
studies by Jungians in other countries, particularly the United
States, have brought the work of Heinz Kohut,[1] Robert Langs[2] and
others[3] into analytical psychology, much to its benefit.

   The springboard for Jungian interest in Harold Searles was an
article by a Jungian analyst, William Goodheart, entitled, 'A
Theory of Analytic Interaction' (1980). Goodheart's intention in
this lengthy book review/treatise was to integrate the work of
Jung, Searles and Langs. His primary focus, however, here and in
subsequent articles (Goodheart, 1984), was on Jung and Langs.
Searles was important but clearly secondary to the other two. As
a result of Goodheart's original three-man discussion, Searles'
work has tended to be linked by Jungians with Langs' theories.[4]

   This Searles/Langs linkage is unfortunate, even if inadvertent.

First, it is erroneous: parallels between Searles and Langs are overestimated. While there are areas of overlap in these two psychoanalysts' theories, their differences are more significant than their similarities.[5] Second and more importantly, this connection with the controversial Langs may deflect Jungians from realizing how close and how complementary is Searles' work to Jung's.[6] More than any of the psychoanalysts in whom Jungians have become interested, Searles has the most to offer analytical psychology, as this book will attempt to show.

In fact, Jungian interest in Searles precedes Goodheart's work by over a decade. Michael Fordham, when discussing delusional (psychotic) transference/countertransference states, was the first to note in print that Searles' work 'complements and expands Jung's description by showing how it feels personally' (1969, p. 283). It is fitting that this initial Jungian mention of Searles should be by Fordham, who for decades was instrumental in furthering Jungian study of countertransference and transference phenomena. During this same era it was Searles who, alongside Racker, Little, Tower, Heimann and other psychoanalysts, pioneered the use of countertransference as a therapeutic instrument.

Interestingly, these psychoanalysts unintentionally were filling in areas that Jung broadly outlined several decades before, perhaps making them what Samuels has termed 'unknowing Jungians' (1985, p. 10). It was probably Jung who introduced the value of a countertransference focus in psychoanalysis. He was the first analyst to insist upon training analysis as a training prerequisite (Jung, 1913; see also Freud, 1912, Ellenberger, 1970, and Roazen, 1976). This was to avoid contamination of the patient – in other words, to avoid countertransference in its classic, 'negative' form. By 1914 Jung was stressing that the analyst's 'personality is one of the main factors in the cure' (1914, p. 260). He refined this further in 1929 by emphasizing that: 1) the 'reciprocal influence' of patient and analyst is unavoidable, 2) 'the doctor is as much "in the analysis" as the patient' and 3) the analyst's emotional reactivity is 'a highly important organ of information' (1929a, pp. 71–2).

These technical areas like analyst/patient reciprocity and countertransference are precisely where Searles' work can be of special help to Jungians. Why? Because Jung's written work, for all its richness, lacks clarity in the clinical domain. Over time Jung's interests, based (understandably enough) on his

2

psychological inclinations and experiences, moved away from the clinical and toward the symbolic/archetypal. Indeed, this symbolic focus and all that goes with it – the collective unconscious, the purposive, the transcendent, the sense of the Self – is one of Jung's great contributions to psychology. And, it should be added, the 'symbolic' approach is both vital for and applicable to clinical work. But the symbolic way is incompletely connected to clinical practice in Jung's writings, even in his case material.[7] In his cases the amplifications are extensive and 'the symbolic life' really does come alive, but the nitty-gritty of the actual analytic work, of the patient's personal life and of the transference is obscure.

Perhaps, as befits Jung's archetypal emphasis, the fascinating power of the symbolic/numinous overrides all else. It is consistent that Jung apparently referred some cases involving personal, reductive or transference work to Toni Wolff (Henderson, 1975). A relevant criticism, or at least one worthy of consideration, has been made by Guntrip, whose viewpoint is in other ways congenial with a Jungian perspective:

> Jung has put his finger on a really determining motive in the psychic life of a human being. It is the inescapable and ineradicable urge to become, and to fulfill oneself as, a person. . . . [But] Jung either does not see, or does not deal with, the question of personal relationship as the medium in which ultimately integration is achieved. . . . One gets the impression that Jung regards integration as an esoteric and wholly internal process, in achieving which we end up inside our own psyche.
>
> (Guntrip, 1961, p. 191)

While Guntrip's critique does not refer to the analytic process *per se* and forgets what Jung said about the necessity of real relationships for 'differentiating' the shadow, anima and so on (1951a), it does speak to an apparent Jungian preference for the 'inner' life over the outer. In a therapy context, this inclination manifests itself in a lack of clinical detail or analyst/patient reference.

In addition, as also befits the 'internalized' nature of Jungian thought, Jung tends to lose the field of mainstream psychology. Jung ians might like to think – and it may be so – that Jung leaves other theorists in the dust. But that only begs the question for those who base their work on Jung and feel he has value for other clinicians.

3

Despite the fair number of 'unknowing Jungians' out there, 'Jung is not yet perceived as a trustworthy figure; there is a credibility gap' (Samuels, 1985, p. 10).

Accordingly, Jung's work (or Jung himself) sometimes gets characterized in textbooks as 'mystical' (which is true in a certain sense) or 'so mysterious as to be almost undiscussable' (Peters, 1962, p. 730), which is not true. Traditional psychoanalysts, of course, usually lambasted Jung during his lifetime, mostly as a result of the acrimonious Freud/Jung split (see Freud, 1914; Glover, 1956; Fromm, 1963). It may also be the case that the whole field of psychology values Jung's work less than does the general 'public', as Misiak and Sexton (1966), Watson (1968) and a Jungian analyst, Mary Ann Mattoon (1981), have pointed out.

In addition to the non-traditional, non-clinical subject matter of his later work – alchemy, eastern religions, synchronicity, etc. – Jung's obscurity and exit from the main current of psychology may be self-inflicted. As he noted, 'I strive quite consciously and deliberately for ambiguity of expression . . . because it reflects the nature of life' (quoted in Jacobi, 1965, p. viii). This chosen ambiguity – combined with what even some Jungians (M. Fordham, 1962; Mattoon, 1981) have acknowledged is Jung's 'less than lucid writing style' (Schultz, 1969, p. 294) – has put the burden of clarification and application of Jung's theories on his followers. While this is a natural legacy to one's successors, a special premium is placed on it in Jung's case because his may be 'the most complex personality theory that exists' (Maddi, 1980, p. 66). Jung in fact seemed to recognize this need for future clarification: when asked why he had not made a more systematic presentation of his work, Jung replied, 'Sorry . . . to complete this psychology would take more than a lifetime' (in Harms, 1962, p. 732).

Jung did what he could during his lifetime, pursuing the subjects his unconscious seemed to insist upon. He followed the psyche into new quarters, essentially numinous though not directly 'clinical.' As Jung himself admitted in a letter:

> You are quite right, the main interest of my work is not concerned with the treatment of the neuroses but rather with the approach to the numinous. But the fact is that the approach to the numinous is the real therapy and inasmuch as you attain to the numinous experiences you are released from the curse of pathology.
>
> (Jung, 1973b, p. 377)

4

This comment by Jung must be taken cautiously, since it is a reaction in a personal letter rather than a published statement on psychotherapy. Nevertheless it typifies both the emphasis of his work and the reason why the therapy world often finds his work inaccessible or impractical.

However, despite all the doubts cast above, there is renewed academic and professional attention to analytical psychology since Jung's death. Maddi's widely used textbook on psychotherapy adds Jung, formerly of 'little contemporary importance' (1980, p. 5), to its second edition, citing a 'groundswell of interest' (p. 66). Hall and Lindszay's well-known text on personality theory emphasizes Jung's 'incalculable influence' on psychology (1978, p. 80). It would appear that the psycho-cultural trends of the '60s,' which fostered 'new' psychologies, re-opened the psychotherapeutic field to Jungian thought. Thus Murphy and Kovach note that 'clinical psychologists of humanistic persuasion have made rich use of Jung' (1972, p. 426). These clinicians, from Rogers to Maslow to Perls, all would appear to be open to, if not consciously influenced by, Jung's purposive, sometimes 'spiritual' conceptions. Even psychoanalytic views of Jung are more charitable in recent decades (Selesnick, 1963; Friedman and Goldstein, 1964; Sandler *et al.*, 1972; Arlow, 1979; Masterson, 1985). Well-known therapists of other persuasions – Carl Whitaker (1981), R.D. Laing (in Evans, 1976), Gene Gendlin (1979) and, amazingly, Albert Ellis (1979) – all stress the value of Jung and their theoretical compatibility with him. Dozens of authors, from diverse orientations, have supplemented or even created their theoretical models using Jung's ideas and methods (see Sedgwick, 1983, for review; also Bibliography in this book).

While extensive use has been made of Jungian ideas to bolster other models of psychotherapy, efforts by Jungians to correct Jungian deficits via other viewpoints have been less frequent. The notable exception is the previously mentioned work by Fordham and other London Jungians, which has stressed developmental approaches, transference/countertransference focus, and the integration of analytical psychology with psychoanalytic theory and method. In approximately the last decade, there has been growing evidence of the influence of the London group on other Jungian training centers worldwide.[8]

Except for the SAP work, until recently the only other significant Jungian study of other schools has been Frey-Rohn's *From Freud to Jung* (1976). Her work is notable because it is extensive, the only book devoted to an in-depth comparison of Jung with another theorist.[9] Nevertheless, while it details differences, it does not directly seek to integrate Jung and Freud, or fill in Jungian deficits as such.

The question arises: Why have there been so few consolidative efforts by Jungians? It cannot be because Jung's work provided all the answers. Even the staunchest 'Jungian' would see room for growth, that being a virtual Jungian credo. And Jung's own life and theorizing showed open-mindedness and continuous movement toward new views and subject matter. Furthermore, the spirit of Jung is distinctly non-traditional, as evidenced by his break from Freud and his resistance to Jung Institutes and 'Jungians' (Jung, 1973b, p. 405). After all, individuation – that combination of multiple factors paradoxically forming a unique 'Self' – is the cornerstone of analytical psychology.

So the answers must lie elsewhere. Practically speaking, Jung's difficult, comprehensive, sometimes obscure theory may itself require 'more than a lifetime' to learn. Also, there are just not that many Jungian analysts (about 300 in 1975, 1500 currently), and many of them are 'lay' analysts, hence not well acquainted with other theories of psychotherapy. Even more simply, many analysts have apparently lacked time or interest in such syntheses. Others may have deemed them unnecessary, or resisted them.

Jung, being human, was probably more gratified by having followers than he let on. He was clearly concerned that his ideas be valued, and perhaps that there be, as he once dreamed, 'The large, waiting crowd' to whom he could give 'the sweet grapes full of healing juices' (1961b, p. 176). A certain closing of ranks naturally formed about him and his ideas, as it did with Freud when Jung left him (and as it would with any small, sometimes embattled band of like-minded pioneers). In addition, it may be difficult to offer innovations to the ideas of the 'founder' while the Great Man is still alive. Jung died in 1961, active until his death, and, except for the SAP, there was a twenty-year lapse before 'Post-Jungian' syntheses were attempted. It was only after Freud's death, for example, that significant neo-Freudian innovations, and splits, evolved. Overall it may be that 'Jungian psychology' is coming out of its more youthful, idealized attachment to the

6

parent/father – separating and individuating. Thus practical, generational and perhaps even oedipal factors may play a part.

As one of the rejecting (and rejected) sons of psychoanalysis, Jung was forced (and wanted) to go his own way. He got what he seemed to need – isolation – to pursue his creative impulses. His near-psychotic inner confrontation with the unconscious formed the basis for his theories and for a new language and understanding of the psyche. Jung's path may have been liberating, but it was lonely – mythic in its solitude. He had no analyst. Accordingly, Jungian theory arose from, and in effect encourages, a private and creative introspection. As Jung said, 'The patient must be alone if he is to find out what it is that supports him when he can no longer support himself. Only this experience can give him an indestructible foundation' (1944, p. 28). Besides this linkage with its own origins and solitary methods, analytical psychology's isolation fits with Jung's general sense of personal isolation from the world, prominent in his childhood and old age (Jung, 1961b, pp. 17, 41–2, 356–8).

For all the above reasons Jungian theory became isolated from other theories, and Jungian access to other theories, which could benefit analytical psychology overall, was restricted. The time to re-join the rest of the (therapy) world has come. Indeed it came first with the London Jungians, and others have followed (Goodheart, Jacoby, Schwartz-Salant).

Harold Searles' work has also suffered from an odd kind of isolation in the analytic community, at least until the 1980s. On the one hand he was seen as 'probably the most widely read and respected authority in the world' on psychotherapy with schizophrenics (Knight, 1965). Strupp (1973) and Coles (1975) hailed his efforts. According to at least one expert, Searles' pioneering work on countertransference – a prime topic today – firmly established his 'place in analytic history' (Langs, in Langs and Searles, 1980, p. 114).

Despite this renown, Searles' work was not much referred to in print, except in small pockets: a computer search in 1982 of *Psychological Abstracts* revealed only two citations where his work was mentioned in any detailed form. This has changed in the last decade, particularly with the massive interest in 'borderline' pathology, about which Searles (1986) has written comprehensively. His work is now frequently cited in wider psychoanalytic contexts.[10] Still, for a long time his work was not well known or accepted, perhaps due to his radical approach to countertransference[11] and perhaps due to his willingness to work with non-medicated schizophrenics.

As the above suggests, Searles is not a classical Freudian analyst. In fact he himself once suggested, 'To the degree that it [analysis] is rigorously classical, it is essentially delusional' (Searles, 1975a, p. 458). Against Freud's dicta, Searles: 1) analyzes schizophrenics, 2) disdains, or at least is dubious about, strict emotional neutrality, and 3) greatly values countertransference. All these are in keeping with 'the widening scope of indications for' and new trends in psychoanalysis, trends in which Searles has led the way.

Not surprisingly Searles has suggested he might be labeled a 'wild analyst' by certain of his peers (1973c, p. 352). If he had developed his ideas in 1912, it is quite possible that he, like Jung, might have had to withdraw from the psychoanalytic movement. In many ways Searles has more in common with psychoanalytic dissenters (Jung, Adler, Rank) or innovators (Klein, Winnicott, Kohut) than with classical Freudians.

Still, Searles is a psychoanalyst of repute, a member of the American Psychoanalytic Association, a training analyst with the Washington Psychoanalytic Institute, and so on. Searles is no Jungian, and Jung of course was not a 'psychoanalyst' after his break from Freud. Undoubtedly Jung was unacquainted with Searles' work, though their careers overlap somewhat. At the same time, while he knows of Jung, Searles has never read Jung directly, only some secondary sources (Searles, personal communication, 1982). There are only three passing references to Jung in all of Searles' writings.

Despite this lack of contact, these two theorists have some interesting areas of biographical overlap, generally speaking. Both share a beginning, if not an end, in classical Freudian analysis. Both began their work with and made important contributions to the understanding of schizophrenia. Searles' work on psychosis continued, of course, resulting in his position of authority. Jung was Eugen Bleuler's assistant when Bleuler coined the term 'schizophrenia,' and Jung was instrumental in early psychological (as opposed to strictly biological) understandings of it. One might say he was 'present at the creation' of the idea of psychotherapy with schizophrenics: in 1903 he conducted the first psychoanalysis of a case of 'dementia praecox' (Jung, 1907). This was the first study to show that schizophrenic content, usually considered simply 'crazy,' had psychological meaning (see Freud, 1914; Fordham, 1978; Satinover, 1984). Therefore these patients could actually be understood. The implications for therapy are vast. Although Jung did not directly continue his research here, his post-Freud theorizing (and personal exploration) also have significant applications to work with schizophrenics.

Not a few have suggested that Jung himself was battling schizophrenia, or at least dealing with his narcissistic wounds or 'psychotic core' via his theories.[12] Searles (who readily admits his one-time 'borderline' propensities, fluidity of identity and occasional envy of patients' psychoses) might well fall into the same category of analysts – those who live and work more from the 'pre-oedipal' than the 'neurotic' zone.

So Searles and Jung, standing somewhat outside the mainstream of analytic theory, practice and personal experience, have more in common than might initially be supposed. The present study will discuss their similarities and differences in detail, aiming toward an integration of their theories. In so doing, another connection between analytical psychology and psychoanalysis can be established, and what might be termed 'contemporary psychoanalysis' (post-Freudian, post-Jungian, post-founding fathers of all sorts) can perhaps be furthered.

Integrative attempts such as this extend well beyond the analytic field. The search for the 'healing factors' in psychotherapy – how and why therapy works – is always of interest, and has even become a hot topic in formal psychological research. In fact the basic question 'Does it work at all?' has only been answered, scientifically speaking, in the last decade or two. Psychotherapy outcome research has proved what was known subjectively, that therapy is effective to a significant degree for most people. The average person (if such exists) gets measurably better in treatment. Smith, Glass and Miller, the authors of the most comprehensive and statistically powerful of this research – they synthesized all known outcome studies – have pointed out that similar healing factors may underlie different therapy models:

> We regard it is clearly possible that all psychotherapies are equally effective, or nearly so. . . . Those elements that unite different types of psychotherapy may be far more influential

than those specific elements that distinguish them.

(1981, pp. 185–6)

Their research and suggestions lend credence to efforts to find the apparently 'nonspecific' sources of healing in analysis and therapy. The present study is such an effort.

2

THEORETICAL
CONSIDERATIONS

Jung and Searles differ in a fundamental way. Jung wrote more about personality than he did about psychotherapy. The opposite is true for Searles: his psychoanalytically-based personality theory receives somewhat less attention than his psychotherapy model.

Yet they have much in common with regard to the origins, sources and applicability of their theories of psychotherapy. Both originally followed Freud. Their theoretical underpinnings were at first, and to some extent still are, in classical psychoanalysis. Both men's theories of psychotherapy are derived primarily from their work with patients (though there is a strong personal component as well). They also draw the not uncommon conclusion that their professional/personal findings are applicable to 'normal' populations. What Searles and Jung discover from their 'ill' clients in psychotherapy forms the basis for their general theories of human personality. Searles for instance states that:

> Research in schizophrenia has its greatest potential value in the fact that the schizophrenic shows us in remarkably etched form that which is so obscured, by years of progressive adaptation to adult personal living, in human beings in general.
>
> (Searles, 1955a, p. 115)

Elsewhere, speaking of 'anxiety concerning change,' Searles says, 'What the therapy of schizophrenia can teach us of the human being's anxiety concerning change, can broaden and deepen our understanding of the nonpsychotic individual also' (1961d, p. 447). In a still later paper Searles (1964) points out the contributions of family therapy to the concept of the healthy family.

11

Jung's view is very much like Searles': 'In mental cases we can observe all the phenomena that are present in normal people, only in a cruder or more enlarged form' (1928a, pp. 143–4). In terms of schizophrenia in particular, Jung states, 'A psychology of the personality lies concealed within psychosis . . . . [there] we encounter the substratum of our own natures' (1961b, p. 127). Jung (1921, 1934a, 1935a) also states that his generally applicable theories of typology, complexes and archetypes are all client-derived in some measure.

Any theory of psychotherapy has implications. First, it implies, even if it denies interest in, a theory of normal personality. That is, a personality theory can always be derived from the principles and practices of a therapy system. Second, there is a 'theory/practice' paradox: a therapist probably needs a theory in order to practice but one cannot wholeheartedly believe or follow a theory until one has practiced it. For Searles and Jung, theory follows practice; and practice is simply based on what is effective. As Jung says regarding the use of fantasy, a central focus of his therapy, 'The real is what works' (1928a, p. 217).

Presenting this theoretical chapter reverses the usual 'theory follows practice' pattern (which in any case is an oversimplification of the ever-changing, cyclic nature of theory-building). Certain general theoretical considerations about personality structure and dynamics will be presented. The practice of psychotherapy, from which these selected aspects of normal personality functioning are empirically derived by Jung and Searles, will be analyzed in later chapters. Although in this book theory precedes practice, the general personality issues presented in this chapter thread their way through the later discussions of psychotherapy itself.

The personified unconscious

The 'unconscious' is a primary theoretical consideration for both Jung and Searles. The dynamic use of this construct, that is, the idea that the unknown and unseen nevertheless have substantive quality and effect, is the essential organizing factor in their theories of psychotherapy.

Describing the unknown as the unconscious reifies it, or makes it a thing. Searles and Jung go further by anthropomorphizing it – they tend to treat it as if it were a person or persons. This personification of the unconscious has many sources, but probably the two most important are the practice of therapy and the phenomenology of fantasy. Only Jung, however, devotes any effort to justifying 'the unconscious' as a concept. He offers as proofs of its existence: the activities of hypnotism and somnambulism, parapraxes (meaningful slips of the tongue, 'Freudian slips'), the creation of dreams, the subliminal existence of memory and ideas, and most importantly, the symptomology of mental illness (Jung, 1931b, pp. 142–3). Searles takes the existence of the unconscious for granted – perhaps the need for a rationale is no longer necessary in his era or for his analytic audience.

Nowhere is the idea of a personified unconscious more clear than in Jung's concept of 'complexes' and Searles' of 'multiple identity processes.' Jung's personality theory was originally known as 'Complex Psychology,' and he proved the theory scientifically by giving patients the *Word Association Test*. Inability, delay or confusion in responding to the stimulus word of the test indicated to Jung that a 'complex' was interfering with a normal response pattern. Something had eclipsed the usual personality, creating a different, alien 'affect-ego' (Jung, 1907, p. 41).

The use of 'affect' in his description of the complex is appropriate. For the complex was originally thought to be the result of a traumatic 'personal matter' (Jung, 1911, p. 599) – something that caused pain and was therefore repressed. The core of the complex then is a painful and even subliminally physiological reaction to some event – a strong 'feeling' in other words. This leads Jung to say that a complex 'has a sort of body' (1935a, p. 72). Like a magnet, this emotional center attracts ideas and associations, some of which are only loosely connected, logically, to the original traumatic event. The complex, then, can be 'constellated' by seemingly random, unimportant events that nevertheless have touched the associative path.

Under repression due to its painful origin and character, this 'sore spot' (Jung, 1931a, p. 528) in the unconscious eventually behaves like an independent personality. Complexes not only have 'body,' independence and power, they ultimately achieve human form as the symbolic 'actors' in dreams (Jung, 1934a, p. 97). The personification of the unconscious psyche by Jung becomes complete when he suggests (1916a, 1928a) that waking consciousness can train itself to converse (active imagination) with these fragmentary personalities of the unconscious, a process resulting in an integration of personality.

Like Jung, Searles gives a scientific name, 'multiple identity processes,' to what he describes phenomenologically as the 'myriad persons' within an individual's internal or unconscious world (1977a, p. 462). And much as Jung found complexes interfering with normal associative processes, Searles finds 'multiple I's' appearing in the language of self-reference. As evidence, Searles notes the conversational use of 'we' or 'us' by patients (as if the person had not one but many selves). Another common verbal clue may be when someone says, 'I don't know where to begin' or 'That wasn't like me' (Searles, 1977a, pp. 464–5) – the usual center of identity has been displaced.

Multiple-identity functioning also appears and becomes known through its effects on the listener. Searles even admits his own countertransference feelings of 'jealousy' about the other person(s) who inhabit an individual's inner world: 'I found this man infuriatingly smug ... he so clearly favored his *self* over *me* that I felt deeply jealous, bitterly left out' (1973a, p. 186). Searles also describes feeling 'outnumbered' by a 'group' or even a 'tribe' of introjects (1977a, p. 470). These rather amusing but also phenomenologically real descriptions by Searles show us that the subjective, unconscious mind is, almost literally, peopled.

This personification of inner life is most evident in dissociated states, particularly psychosis. Searles notes that in schizophrenic conditions not just the inner world, but the outer world of perception, may consist of hallucinated introjects of 'tangibly real ... biological literalness' (1964, p. 724). This is reminiscent of Jung's statement that in psychosis it is the complexes, now liberated from conscious control, that become 'visible and audible' (1935a, p. 72).

But despite the fact that multiple-identity processes are most readily seen in extreme psychopathology, Searles suggests that in all patients, 'Introjects have the subjective personal-identity value, and interpersonal impact, of persons' (1973a, p. 184). Less disturbed, neurotic patients also have 'persons' within. Ultimately, Searles' opinion is that even the normal person's sense of personal identity is of the same quality:

I have come to see that the healthy individual's sense of identity is far from being monolithic in nature. It involves, rather, myriad internal objects functioning in lively and

14

harmonious interaction . . . but does not involve their being congealed into so unitary a mass as I once thought.

(Searles, 1977a, p. 462)

In this most recent stage of his theoretical evolution, Searles seems to be questioning the idea of clearly demarcated ego/unconscious boundaries, and perhaps even the assumed power superiority of ego-consciousness over the unconscious. Certainly human personality is no longer viewed by Searles as a unified, predictable whole. The sense of 'self' is a more flexible, divergent pheno- menon, consisting more of a consistent self-awareness than a steady, static self *per se*.

For Jung as well as Searles, the idea of personality as a united, conscious whole is questionable. The complexes turn out to be not just momentarily constellated 'splinter psyches' but rather the unknown, 'focal and nodal points' of the psyche (Jung, 1931a, p. 529). They form the foundations of the personality. From Jung's perspective the development of personality (or what Searles terms the 'sense of identity') consists of a multiplicity of complexes coming into contact with the conscious 'ego.' It should be noted that Jung's 'ego' is also a complex, but a stronger one (Jung, 1907, p. 40) characterized by the sense of continuity in one's physical presence ('my' body), ongoing memory and consciousness (Jung, 1951a).

Origins of the unconscious

The question naturally arises of the origin of the 'persons' within. Jung's (1920) original postulate was that complexes were induced externally and were traumatic at the core. Over time, he saw the nucleus of the complex as consisting of a predisposition as well as an outer, actual experience of person or event. This idea of predisposition is connected, of course, with Jung's (1936a) concept of the archetypes – the timeless, universal modes of experiencing, perceiving and symbolizing that are shared by all individuals. In the formation of the complex, the internal inclination (the archetype or predisposition) meets with and colors the external situation. The mechanism of this interaction is not precisely defined by Jung but, as his great emphasis on the 'collective unconscious' indicates, the internal dimension is as important as the objective event.

15

Jung's elevation of the complex to collective, archetypal status has no direct equivalent in Searles' work. For Searles, the development of a personal identity, however pluralistic, seems to lie in the sphere of external, or at least interpersonal, causation. Healthy ego-formation begins with a mutually dependent and caring, 'preambivalent symbiosis' between mother and child (Searles, 1958b, 1961g). Out of this undifferentiated phase evolves a series of unconscious identifications between the infant and his family, particularly the mother and father. The 'part-aspects' of their personalities are incorporated or introjected by the child (Searles, 1951, 1959a). In effect, the child takes on the multifaceted personality components of the parents – an external source therefore of the 'myriad persons' composing a person's identity. Thus it appears that the outer, 'objective' origins of personality formation receive greater emphasis from Searles than Jung. This is consistent with other aspects of their theorizing.

Subject/object questions

Despite Searles' above-mentioned focus on external sources, the subjective element is inherent in his description and in some of his later comments. First, for axiomatic reasons, the ability to introject the outside world implies the subjective capability to receive it. Jung extends Searles in this respect by theorizing directly about innate capacities and modes – the archetypes – of interpreting psychological experience. Searles does not make clear if the introjector's unconscious is an active or passive participant in the introjection process.

But Searles does assert throughout his writings (1951, 1961e, 1963b, 1964, 1965b) that the subjective interpretation of events holds sway over their actual reality. In his first, published article, for example, Searles suggests that a person's apparently interpersonal relationship with his mother is really an 'intrapersonal' relationship:

> This 'mother' has not been the real mother, not the mother who exists in the reality outside himself, but rather a fantasy figure constructed largely of repressed and projected aspects of his personality which are as yet intolerable to the ego.
>
> (Searles, 1951, p. 47)

In a later work (perhaps using the same client as an example?) Searles says, 'It came as a surprise to see that the real mother, as a denizen of outer reality, was less important ... than was the intrapsychic early-mother imago, the early-mother introject' (1964, p. 719). Searles goes on to warn: 'It is not basically the mother or father, for example, who is central to the patient's illness, but rather the patient's introject, distorted and un-integrated into his ego, of that parent' (p. 730).

Searles' (1961g, 1968) use, then, of the terminology 'Good Mother' and 'Bad Mother,' while reflecting the experience of the infant, seems to correspond more than just verbally to Jung's (1911–12/1952) description of the ambivalence of the mother archetype: 'the loving and the terrible mother,' or the 'great mother'/'devouring mother.' And what Searles terms the 'confusion of narcissistic processes with true object relations' (1964, p. 720), or mistaking the intrapsychic for the interpersonal, is explicit in Jung's 'complex' theory. Jung likewise says:

> The image we form of a human object is, to a very large extent, subjectively conditioned. In practical psychology, therefore, we would do well to make a rigorous distinction between the image or *imago* of a man and his real existence.
> (Jung, 1921, p. 73)

Not only is the image subjective, but it may be essentially incorrect; hence, the need for 'rigorous distinction.' The image/reality discrepancy is also implicit in Jung's theory of impersonal, independent organizers of fantasy and perception – the archetypes. Jung states as much in the following example, recalling Searles' discussion of the real mother vs. the 'early-mother imago' (1964, p. 719):

> Up till now everybody has been convinced that the idea 'my father,' 'my mother,' etc., is nothing but a factual reflection of the real parent. ... X's idea of the father is a complex quality for which the real father is only in part responsible, an indefinitely larger share falling to the son. So true is this that every time he criticizes or praises his father he is unconsciously hitting back at himself.
> (Jung, 1951a, p. 18)

In other words Jung, like Searles, is concerned here with projection.

What both theorists (Searles, 1958a, p. 213; Jung, 1934a, p. 96) have identically called 'foreign bodies' in the psyche have now

17

evolved into the cornerstones of a radical theory of human personality. The separate selves within have a large measure of autonomy, operating either totally independently or, at best, in loose harmony with the 'ego.' Though theoretically originating in actual, outer realities, these inner selves quickly seem to develop their own separate worlds in accord with the individual's private subjectivity. Both authors conclude that it is reasonably normal for an individual to be composed of several quasi-personalities. Thus the idea of the individual in any traditional, monistic sense has been superseded in Jung's and Searles' pluralistic phenomenology.

Phylogenetic inheritance

Again, the only key difference between Jung's 'complex theory' and Searles' 'multiple-identity processes' seems to lie in Jung's archetypal vs. Searles' personalistic view of their sources. But even here the points of overlap are striking when the background of their theories is explored. It appears that Searles has also incorporated elements of a phylogenetic theory of man within his generally personalistic view of the origin of identity. That is, an individual's psychological development is thought to re-trace the psychological evolution of the human race generally.

In his only purely theoretical work, *The Nonhuman Environment*, Searles stresses that psychology has explored in depth the nature of interpersonal and intrapersonal processes, but has ignored the equally 'transcendental importance' of the nonhuman realm (1960, p. 6). Searles' interest in this latter area stems from his own nostalgic feelings about nature and also from the subjective experiences of many of his psychotic patients (e.g., 'I am a machine . . . a stone . . . God').

Schizophrenic experience in fact is one proof Searles offers for his phylogenetic theory of ego development. He also believes that a child's psychological growth follows a sequence from inorganic to animate to human. In other words, the newborn is so entirely merged with the world that it is not yet subjectively human or alive. The infant gradually realizes, unconsciously in part, that he is alive (not inanimate), then humanly alive (not a plant or animal). Throughout life, however, the original connection to the nonhuman world remains one of a person's most treasured (and feared) modes of existence.

As further evidence of this 'ontogeny follows phylogeny' hypothesis, Searles (1960) cites the powerful emotional chords struck in people by the theory of evolution. He also mentions creation myths and the easy, human-to-nonhuman inter-changeability in almost all mythological stories. The individual's unconscious would seem to resonate not only with the personified introjects discussed earlier, but nonpersonal ones or, as Searles calls them, 'a multitude of inanimate objects' (p. 49).

One of Jung's most controversial theories, his hypothesis of a 'collective unconscious' in each individual, is fundamentally a phylogenetic theory. He suggests that the mind, like the body, has a layered, evolutionary history (Jung, 1935a, 1953b). Archaic, ancestral and primitive modes of thinking and apperception – the archetypes – are passed on from generation to generation. According to Jung:

> This whole psychic organism corresponds exactly to the body. . . . Theoretically, it should be possible to 'peel' the collective unconscious, layer by layer, until we come to the psychology of the worm, or even the amoeba.
>
> (Jung, 1931b, p. 152)

Just as the body evolves in interaction with the physical world,

> . . . the same is true of the psyche. Its peculiar organization must be intimately connected with environmental conditions. . . . From the collective unconscious, as a timeless and universal psyche, we should expect reactions to universal and constant conditions, whether psychological, physiological, or physical.
>
> (Jung, 1931b, p. 152)

Thus the psyche is an evolutionary, phylogenetic concept.

Infantile personality development, according to Jung (1928d), begins in a stage of rather dreamlike, almost nonhuman unconsciousness. The child is psychologically similar to an animal, though with archetypal human potentiality. Gradually, primitive and archaic modes of existence predominate, and the infant's world becomes, in effect, the world of the collective unconscious. Thus, until the first glimmers of ego-consciousness arise, the child exists in a primordial, fantasy world – a position which is comparable to Searles' descriptions. As Searles suggests, the infant's objective world is 'undifferentiated' and 'animism' precedes any sense of personal aliveness (1960, p. 52). Jung (1911–12/1952, 1931d, 1931e) says much the same thing, even using the same words as Searles when describing the pre-logical thinking of very young children, primitive peoples and ancient man. That the child's ontology is following phylogeny must be a direct implication of the child's preconscious immersion in the collective unconscious. Jung ultimately states this explicitly: 'In accordance with phylogenetic law, we still recapitulate in childhood reminiscences of the prehistory of the race and of mankind in general' (1931d, p. 32).

Thus, as implied in the idea of subjectively overdetermined introjects or complexes, the personification of the unconscious for both theorists is more than personally determined. It is historically and even prehistorically determined. Strikingly, Searles and Jung use many of the same proofs for the phylogeny argument. Searles in *The Nonhuman Environment* invokes mythology, anthropology, fairy tales, dreams, hallucinations and therapy with schizophrenics as evidence for man's belief in human–nonhuman metamorphosis and interchangeability. These are precisely the empirical facts whose universality and parallelism Jung (1911–12/1952, 1919, 1931d, 1954b) uses in support of his hypothesis of a 'collective unconscious.'

The chief Searles–Jung differences in the phylogeny area seem to be ones of emphasis or degree. Searles, for instance, traces infantile phylogenetic development all the way back to an inorganic state. Jung's view of human psychological evolution seems only to hypothesize a potential relationship to invertebrate animal states (e.g., the amoeba). However, Jung (1941, 1950b, 1951a) does point to quasi-inanimate states at, so to speak, the other end of personality development: the constellation of the 'Self' can be symbolized by plant forms, geological, astronomical, geometrical and supra-human 'God' images. A very similar point is made by Searles: 'The most significant of human growth experiences are portrayed, in the unconscious, by such nonhuman symbols as plants and animals' (1960, p. 264).

Although Searles does dare to go farther down the phylogenetic scale, he is perhaps more tentative than Jung about its implications. Jung, after all, develops an entire theory of human personality based on archetypal considerations. Searles aims lower, and his phylogenetic view is secondary to his discussion of the nonhuman environment. He is quick to point out that ontogeny follows phylogeny in only a subjective sense. An infant's passage through earlier evolutionary states occurs so early in life that it is *as if* the infant were really pre-human. For Searles this is the only rational and 'scientifically tenable view' – anything else would imply a belief in reincarnation and the actual unconscious memory of experience as some sort of lower life form (1960, p. 265). Thus, Searles' phylogeny argument always stays reasonably close to the ontogeny argument.

By stressing the archetypal dimension, Jung is not so bound to ontogeny, but neither does he take phylogeny as far back into the inorganic world as Searles does. In fact, Jung has the same opinion as Searles on reincarnation: 'The idea of a former existence is a projection of the psychological condition of early childhood' (1935a, p. 95). On the other hand, Jung (1928a) theorizes that archetypal proclivities are the result of repeated historical experiences that have been imprinted or stamped on the unconscious mind. This is close to the concept Searles rejects of a specific memory inheritance. But Jung, again, does not delve much into lower life forms, except for his theoretical exposition on 'invertebrate' layers (Jung, 1931a, p. 152). He stays closer to human, though primitive, modalities. Jung (1949a, 1961a) also emphasizes that archetypes prescribe form but not specific content to perception and fantasy. Thus he avoids the Lamarckian mistake of postulating inheritance of actual memories from generation to generation. Archetypes are ancestrally forged potentialities and structures rather than specific recollections.

As it turns out, Searles' and Jung's different foci in the realm of prehuman experience come together in their discussion of 'phylogenetic regression' (see next chapter). Meanwhile, their shared view of the unconscious as personified, subjective rather than objective, and evolutionarily determined, leads to further theoretical considerations.

Psychological 'reality'

Implicit in Searles' and Jung's theories is the belief that psychic reality has a place virtually equal to that of objective reality. For example, when in the 'scientific' mode, Jung (1946) states that nothing can be definitely said about the unconscious because it is simply unknown, an inference. All statements about it are 'as if' statements (Jung, 1935a, p. 9).

On the other hand, it is evident from Jung's theories, religious interests and personal experiences that the unconscious is more than a hypothetical derivative. It possesses absolute reality. Therefore Jung calls it the 'objective psyche' (1917, p. 66). It is a real, 'inner' world, containing psychic 'objects' accessible via fantasy, just as the outer world contains material objects accessible through the senses (Jung, 1928a, p. 218). Fantasy, therefore, can be as important as reality. Jung characterizes this 'discovery of the reality of the psyche and the overcoming of rationalistic psychologism' in strong terms:

> For those who are vouchsafed such a discovery, the psyche appears as something objective, a psychic non-ego. This discovery is very like the discovery of a new world. . . . This tremendous experience means a shattering of foundations, an overturning of our arrogant world of consciousness, a cosmic shift of perspective, the true nature of which can never be grasped rationally or understood in its full implications.
>
> (Jung, 1932, p. 763)

Therefore, the objective psyche is literally 'out of this world,' and into another. For Jung, the unconscious is real, alive. It is no surprise, though it is inaccurate, that Jung has been called mystical, non-scientific (Schultz, 1969) or even temporarily (though creatively) mentally ill (Ellenberger, 1970; Brome, 1978).

It is from the 'mentally ill' that Searles derives much evidence for his very similar view of psychic reality. He states his opinion in a manner that at first seems paradoxical: the acutely psychotic patient has, 'subjectively, no imagination' (Searles, 1962a, p. 574). By this Searles means that there is no separation between imagination and reality, and therefore no recognition of fantasy as such. The symbolic world overwhelms the objective world, such that a schizophrenic may experience what the 'normal' person metaphorically expresses (e.g., 'walking on quicksand,' 'feeling blue,' etc.). Fantasy is literally perceived, and no more definitive statement about the reality of the psyche could be made.

The question that arises is: Does this apply to normal experience of the unconscious as well? As in the ontogeny/ phylogeny discussion above, Searles stays closer to the rationally tenable than Jung. Whereas Jung simply forges ahead, giving inner and outer realms equal reality, Searles' view of psychic reality must be inferred. Since it is clear that the unconscious is real to the schizophrenic, and since Searles (1955a, 1961d) feels that schizophrenic findings apply to normal functioning, it follows that the unconscious may be real, though less visible, in all people. In a less logical vein, Searles' description of the 'interpersonal impact' of internal objects implies measurable effects and therefore real existence (1973a, p. 184). Likewise, Searles' (1958a) discussion of the influence of the presumably normal therapist's unconscious processes on the client suggests the inductive effects (hence, psychic reality) of the normal unconscious. Finally, Searles' tremendous emphasis on therapist–patient interchanges, transformations and cure via unconscious mechanisms certainly would seem to imply the potent reality of the unconscious.

Unconscious dynamics and communications

This phenomenological, psychic reality of 'selves' in the unconscious gives rise to general considerations about unconscious dynamics. The pluralistic personality is not only 'populated,' but that population appears to be exceedingly mobile. This is true not only in the intrapersonal domain of ego/unconscious relations, but in interpersonal relations as well.

What Searles calls the 'interpersonal impact' (1973a, p. 184) of internal objects or Jung (1909, 1935a) calls the contagiousness of complexes are founded on highly complex dynamics of unconscious communication between people. These communications seem to rest on mechanisms typically termed introjection and projection. Closely allied are processes of 'identity' or 'identification' between people. Introjection has already been discussed in terms of the origins of complexes and multiple-identity processes: somehow a person internalizes other people, particularly the family or emotional situations closely connected to the family. This introjection undergoes subjective modifications such that an internal 'imago,' rather than a necessarily accurate replica of reality, is formed. Projection also has previously been mentioned, with regard to the subjective basis of personality. Projection takes these imagos or internal objects and thrusts them out into the world. The different 'selves' of the pluralistic personality may then get attributed to actual people in the environment.

23

Although presented sequentially, it is not clear if introjection precedes projection or vice versa. There appears to be some continuous interaction: subjective elements are projected onto incoming, external realities in the introjection process. Hence, 'imagos' are not necessarily correct representations. At the same time, subjective predispositions toward imago-formation could not be called into play without introjecting reality first. External reality has some sort of catalytic effect.

The precise mechanisms involved in these hypothetical processes – how 'selves' crystallize and how they are sensed and interchanged – seem to be unfathomable. All Jung (1935a) and Searles (1961b) can finally say is that the exact details are unconscious, hence unknown, and that the processes take place somehow via the unconscious.

For instance, Searles (1958a) remarks that an individual may introject not only conscious but also unconscious aspects of another person. This is especially true of children, of course, as they form from parents the internal imagos upon which enduring personal identity is based. But how can a child do this? Surely he cannot consciously decipher the conscious, much less the unconscious, complexity of an adult. Says Searles (1958b), the unconscious does it.

Similarly, Jung speaks of 'intuition' as a normal function in all people, defining it as 'perception . . . via the unconscious' (1935a, p. 15). People and things are sensed and understood without knowing how or why. This unconscious, intuitive comprehension of things has vast implications for psychotherapy. For the moment, it should be noted that Searles (1958a, p. 214) and Jung (1921, p. 425) both consider introjection to be the basis of 'empathy.'

The importance of introjective/projective processes for Searles and Jung cannot be overestimated. These mechanisms, however indescribable at the core, not only form the building blocks of personality – they are involved in the continuous experience of the world and life in general. As Searles states:

> Man's identity enables him to perceive the world not merely by mirroring it, but, at a symbiotic level or relatedness, by literally sampling it through processes of introjection and projection.
>
> (Searles, 1966–7, p. 67)

24

According to Jung, man starts off in an original state of unconscious 'identity' with the world until projections are understood and introjected back into the subject (1921, p. 441). Prior to that, person and world are undifferentiated. This forms the basis for Jung's statement that projection turns the world 'into a replica of one's own unknown face' (1951a, p. 9).

It is not surprising then that communication between people can be a very complicated affair. Introjection and projection distort reality and relationships in some ways, but they also permit a kind of subliminal communication between people. According to Jung and Searles, a fundamental type of communication happens through the unconscious. As noted earlier, the more permanent aspects of personality are formed via identifications, projections and introjections. However, these processes also play a role in more transitory interpersonal engagements. Whereas physical and conscious boundaries (i.e., 'ego boundaries') are self-evident, it seems that lines of demarcation between people are more blurred at an unconscious level.

This is the level of 'symbiotic' involvement between people to which Searles (1966–7) refers. Jung (1926) describes it as a sort of atmospheric condition, potentially contaminating: one soaks up or breathes in the psychological atmosphere of a person or place. For Jung and Searles both, it is as if people can have a subtle, underlying bondedness or emotional connection that belies any outward boundaries. It might be compared to radiation – invisible, scarcely measurable, but powerful.

In addition, Searles (1965b) and Jung (1907) postulate an affective basis of personality that is intimately tied to these complex processes. That is, the source of the potent *effects* of unconscious communications is their *affective* basis. What are transferred through the symbiotic, common ground between people are emotions – not images alone but the feelings and conflicts that go with them.

Interpersonal relationships are thus clouded by subjective and mostly unconscious processes. The implication is that objective reality is interpreted, if not distorted, by an individual in unique ways. At this juncture, however, both theorists seem to make an 'about-face.' Although projection creates misperceptions of reality, Jung and Searles suggest that projections can be accurate as well.

Searles, after finding 'basically intrapsychic processes at work in ostensibly interpersonal relationships,' goes on to admit that virtually all his writings emphasize just the opposite (1965b, p. 33). Even in his first professional paper, Searles insists on the 'reality basis' of projections and defines projections as distortions in degree but not in quality (1949/79, p. 181). They are in many ways more fundamentally correct than incorrect, as he repeatedly acknowledges (Searles, 1949/79, 1958a, 1963b, 1967a, 1972a).

In light of an individual's ability to unconsciously introject unconscious aspects of another person (Searles, 1958a), the issue of what is 'true' grows hazy. Is a person distorting when projecting, or accurately 're-projecting' the introject of the other person back onto that person?

Jung's formulations raise the same question. For all his talk of predisposition and archetypal subjectivity, Jung also states:

> Experience shows that the carrier of the projection is not just *any* object but is always one that proves adequate to the nature of the content projected – that is to say, it must offer the content a 'hook' to hang on.
>
> (Jung, 1946, p. 291)

So, projection and reality are not as far apart as predicted, and Jung is postulating much the same thing as Searles. Furthermore, the projector may sense unknown parts of another person, in which case the latter may have unconsciously 'lured out' the projection.[1] This is all the more easy because in the Jungian view both projector and projectee will possess parallel, human potentialities (archetypes). Articulating the interpersonal/ intrapersonal problem still further, Jung adds that projections can only be realized in the context of an actual relationship (1951a, p. 22). That is, not only will they first be found there (Jung, 1935a), but they must continually have an interpersonal context as a foil to their own, subjective reality.

Polarities

As the above discussion indicates, Jung and Searles feel relatively at ease with contradictory or at least paradoxical viewpoints. Logical consistency means less to them than factual empiricism. If the facts happen to be, for example, that projections can be both delusional and accurate, then so be it. By the same token, truth is not any one thing and may lie in the realm of paradox or outside the limits of causality.

It is not surprising, then, that what Searles calls 'ambivalence' or Jung calls 'the opposites' are woven into their theories. Searles sees ambivalence at the heart of individuation (1961g), identity-formation (1966b), psychopathology (1961d) and the patient–therapist relationship (1973a). It is perhaps the fundamental, underlying structure in his theory. Jung also writes, 'I see in all that happens the play of opposites' (1929a, p. 337), and one sees in his work a constant dichotomizing around conscious/ unconscious, good/evil, rational/irrational, instinct/spirit, etc. The index to his *Collected Works* lists 119 pairs of opposites. His theories of individuation, typology, Self, archetypes and dream interpretation (to name but a few) are all dialectically oriented.

Consciousness

The dialectical bases of much of Jung's and Searles' theorizing, combined with their vision of human personality as pluralistic and fluid, give rise to a further similarity. Both authors emphasize the great importance of consciousness, while de-emphasizing its active power.

The importance of consciousness seems to lie in the area of simple awareness or 'self'-consciousness, rather than will or force. Searles points out, for example, that maturation involves an increased ability to experience a wide range of emotions, not the ability to restrict or eliminate the distasteful ones (1949/79, 1966a). In effect, one observes and allows one's many selves to fully express themselves to oneself. The personification of the unconscious naturally lends itself to this sort of 'self'-discovery. As Searles writes:

> I have come to believe that the more healthy an individual is, the more consciously does he live in the knowledge that there are myriad 'persons' – internal objects each bearing some sense-of-identity value – within him.
>
> (Searles, 1977a, p. 462)

The sense of identity is not exactly fragmented here, but it is expressed in terms of a versatile awareness, not some consistently predictable 'me.'

Jung places great emphasis on consciousness as a significant step in the history of mankind and of any individual (1928a, 1940). He is also fond of the analogy between consciousness and light, in the sense that consciousness sheds light on the dark world of the unconscious (Jung, 1944, 1954a). Since the collective unconscious is of such primary importance and extends to infinite depths, the searchlight of consciousness becomes doubly important to Jung.

However, the primacy of consciousness for Jung is only so for the reason that it permits the integration of the unconscious. The position of consciousness *vis-à-vis* personified complexes is to stand back, 'let go,' and allow fantasy to express itself (Jung, 1950a). This gives complexes an importance equal to ego processes, and then permits the ego to listen and respond to the unconscious. Consciousness is not exactly passive here, but it is receptive and relinquishes control of the autonomous personalities within. Through this process, says Jung:

> We find that thoughts, feelings and affects are alive in us which we would never have believed possible . . . those who do succeed can hardly fail to be impressed by all the ego does not know and never has known.
>
> (Jung, 1951a, p. 19)

As with Searles' theory, the ego discovers the self. In fact, as Jung delves further into his own definition of 'Self,' the sense of personal identity is seen as shifting to a 'midpoint' somewhere between the unconscious/conscious or inner/outer worlds (1928a, p. 221). Ego-consciousness, while the seat of the 'empirical personality' (Jung, 1951a, p. 3), becomes somewhat secondary to the 'total personality' (p. 5) or Self, except insofar as it is necessary to mediate the Self's emergence.

Self and individuation

The preceding paragraphs point to another issue. Searles and Jung frequently use the same words when describing personality phenomena. But homonyms are not necessarily synonyms. Two key terms in the Searles–Jung vocabulary, 'self' and 'individuation,' have already arisen. They are of central importance in each author's theory.

Both writers have similarly receptive, awareness-oriented attitudes toward the self. But what each means by 'self' is different in important respects. The difference is well epitomized by the way each spells the word: for Searles it is 'self,' for Jung it is often 'Self.'

Searles' self is not usually defined as a unitary concept. It is often spoken of in the plural, as 'selves' (Searles, 1973a, 1977a). This has particular reference to its unconscious, multiple-identity aspect as assorted, internal objects. But Searles (1961e) sometimes uses it singularly, with reference to one's individual self or sense of self. It is closest here to his descriptions of a 'personal identity' (Searles, 1966–7). In fact, just as the many selves within are described as 'multiple-identity' processes, it is fair to say that 'self' and 'identity' in the singular are approximately interchangeable in Searles' work. Whether multiple or singular, the self is a fluid phenomenon, even an organ of perception whose vicissitudes are informative (Searles, 1977a).

Aside from these changing, barometric qualities, Searles' description of the self has two other distinct features. First, it is an entirely human conception. Despite its phylogenetic evolution and its ongoing tie with the nonhuman world (Searles, 1965b), the self is essentially formed out of parental models and human introjects. Second, the evolution of the self is not such that it ever becomes an enduring unity, though it does have a relatively consistent quality. Hence, self-acceptance, for Searles, seems to involve a surrender of permanent self-image in favor of increasing comfort with the variety of part-aspects that compose one's identity. Ideally, one's inner diversity appears as strength rather than 'threatened insanity' (Searles, 1977a, p. 462).

Jung's 'Self' has a transcendent quality that is in keeping with its frequent capitalization. His conception has to do with the 'wholeness' of the personality, which again for Jung is something more than the 'empirical' personality (1951a, p. 3). That is, the whole personality is the sum total and synthesis of conscious and unconscious. This definition is colored by Jung's postulate of a boundless, collective unconscious, too: if the unconscious is infinite, then the Self is infinite, accordingly. And if the unconscious is impersonal as well as personal, then one's Self has impersonal elements.

This nonpersonal, elevated characteristic is best exhibited by Jung's experiential descriptions of the Self. Because of its unconscious components, complete Selfhood is, by definition, approachable but not realizable. Yet, along the path of Self-realization, the Self may be subjectively felt or grasped. Though this experience is basically 'inexpressible,' Jung suggests parallels with the religious experience of 'Christ within' or the oriental concept of the Tao (1928a, p. 221). The main phenomenological feature is not 'I live' but 'it lives me' (Jung, 1929b, p. 132) – i.e., the person or ego is felt to be the object of a superior force. Elsewhere, Jung states that symbols of the Self and of God are the same (1951a, 1958b). A feeling of divinity or 'numinosity' is prevalent. Thus the Self's transcendent, ungraspable nature is confirmed in Jung's work.

Obviously, Jung's idea of the Self moves into the realm of metaphysical or religious experience and at this point differences with Searles' lower-case self arise. As previously explained, Searles' self is an entirely human concept, while Jung's has spiritual connotations. Furthermore, because Jung's unconscious takes on such massive, collective proportions – such that persons may be burdened by historical as well as personal matters (Jung, 1936a, 1961b) – Jung's view of Self is on a similarly vast scale. Searles' self has more personalistic, less world-wide implications. He also seems to question the visionary experience that could be involved in Jung's theory. According to Searles, mystical experience is usually a regression to 'infantile-omnipotent' states (1960, pp. 107–8) in which personal identity has dissolved into disguised 'Good Mother' or 'Bad Mother' recollections (depending on the positive or negative flavor of the transcendent experience). Similarly, religious experiences, which to Jung (1958d) are not necessarily abnormal, hint of pathology to Searles (1960). Overall, whereas Jung is ready to go 'beyond science' (1928a, p. 240), Searles stays closer to the 'scientifically tenable' (1960, p. 265). Searles' self is related to 'personal identity'; Jung's is related to God.

Jung's Self is also more closely connected to the notion of synthesis than Searles' is. Both theorists postulate a pluralistic personality and a dialectical framework. For Jung, the diverse elements of personality and the clash of opposites are united by the emergence in symbolic form of the transcendent 'third' thing, the Self (1946, p. 199). The Self is generally considered by Jung to be a special, 'central' archetype that eventually creates order amidst the chaos of complexes and other, lesser archetypes (1958d, p. 734). Jung calls it a compensation for the dialectical dilemma of personality (1928a). In Searles' system there is no such compensatory reward for conflict. One's sense of self remains a sense of many, internal 'selves,' which function in a relatively 'harmonious interrelatedness' (Searles, 1977a, p. 462). There is no ultimate unification in anything like a greater, symbolic Self.

Selfhood is closely linked with the process of 'individuation' for Jung and Searles. Again, in certain respects both theorists mean the same thing by 'individuation,' but their contexts are different. According to Searles, individuation is a process which denotes the establishment of some sort of separate identity after a period of symbiotic relatedness (1961g). His context is specifically the early, parent–child relationship. The emergence of the individual self involves not only liberation from but a foundation in a mutually incorporative, adoring, mother–child symbiosis (Searles, 1966–7). The individuation of the self results from the realization of ambivalence and the nevertheless painful foregoing of the symbiotic bond.

This individuation process, however, is not a one-time, linear process, according to Searles. The capacity for fusion between self and others (and world) remains 'the dynamic substrate of adult living' (Searles, 1973a, p. 177). An individual is destined to undergo a continual re-individuation process in addition to a simultaneous symbiosis–individuation experience. That is, a symbiotic relationship to the world always exists at unconscious levels (Searles, 1966–7).

What individuation ultimately means – and evidently it is something quite paradoxical – is never fully explained by Searles. His emphasis throughout his work is predominantly on symbiosis. As he readily admits, 'It is surely no coincidence that I've never gotten to write a definitive paper – definitive for me – on individuation. I keep putting that off for one reason or another' (Searles, 1980, p. 108).

One person who does attempt to define 'individuation' is Jung. It means 'coming to selfhood' or 'self realization' (Jung, 1928a, p. 173), in the previously mentioned context of a quasi-transcendent Self. But this Self is very different than Searles'. And whereas Searles basically stresses the childhood aspect of individuation, Jung (1931c, 1931f) stresses that it is an adult endeavor. In fact, to pursue Self-actualization before age thirty-five or forty is, to Jung, 'almost a sin, or at least a danger' (1931f, p. 399). Issues of social adaptation and ego consolidation must more or less be solved before questions about life's meaning and one's true personality can be undertaken.

31

Jungian individuation also presupposes a relativization of the ego which is in contrast to the establishment of ego-identity that occurs in Searles' version. From a boundaryless mother–child tie comes a feeling of individual identity for the individuating child, according to Searles. Jung (1928d, p. 54) seems to be referring to a similar thing in much less detail when he speaks of a child's first experience of himself as 'I' (i.e., I am a person). Nevertheless, ego consolidation, which at any rate takes place gradually in Jung's system, is not what he means by individuation. Jungian individuation entails the already established ego assuming a somewhat subordinate position in relation to the Self (Jung, 1954a). The ego is not displaced or shattered, and consciousness always remains paramount, but the person's ego 'now appears as the object of that which works within him' (Jung, 1931f, p. 49). This superior, 'internal agent' is the Self. Thus, in individuation the center of personality is no longer identical with the ego but shifts to what Jung envisions as a 'mid-point' between the conscious and unconscious (1928a, p. 221).

Despite their different formulations of the nature and timing of individuation, Searles and Jung share some areas of congruence. For example, in spite of all his emphasis on childhood, Searles also believes that complete individuation is never achieved. The symbiosis-to-individuation paradigm is apparently lifelong. Searles says:

> A healthy adult, too, lives a daily and yearly life which involves, in its most essential ingredients, experiences – whether measured in moments or phases of life – of symbiotic relatedness and reindividuation.
>
> (Searles, 1973a, p. 177)

It is not clear whether the initial individuation from mother–child symbiosis is the most important of many, the prototype for all the subsequent re-individuations, or simply one of many. Searles usually stresses the first, mother–child one, perhaps because he also locates psychopathology there (see next chapter). Still, Searles' attitude in this instance is closer to Jung's belief that individuation is an adult matter. It also echoes Jung's opinion that the path and not the goal of individuation is what is important, because the Self can never be fully realized (1934d, 1946). Jung also mentions that in the archetypal myth of the hero, which represents the triumph of consciousness (hero) over the unconscious (darkness, dragon, etc.), the hero's task is never done (1911–12/1952). He must always return.

Jung picks up the childhood motif, too, but in a strictly symbolic way. The individuation process for Jung promotes the birth of the Self or the 'rebirth' of personality, in the sense of the individual's rejuvenating discovery of a preconscious, pre-existent wholeness (1939a, p. 114). The Self is often symbolized by the appearance of the 'eternal' or 'divine' child (Jung, 1940, pp. 170, 178). This child archetype is the 'new' thing, the first inkling and anticipation of the future totality. In a parallel way in the symbolism of alchemy, which for Jung (1944, 1946) is a metaphor for the individuation process, the youthful *filius philosophorum* (philosopher's son) is the goal of the 'opus' and symbol of the synthesis of the Self. Youth also plays a role in Jungian individuation in that a paradisal, undifferentiated unity of personality may exist in the young infant (Jung, 1931c). In this naturally whole but slumbering state, the 'opposites' which form the dialectical ground of personality have not yet divided. Soon, life and conflicts begin. The individuating adult re-unites these opposites and is reborn into this original sense of totality, but in a conscious way. Thus, the symbol of the child or youth points backwards to this dimly recalled infantile reality and forwards to the conscious rebirth of wholeness (Jung, 1940).

From the above it is clear that Jung often speaks of individuation as an act mediated by symbols and fantasy, while Searles refers to it more literally as a separation of the mother and child. Yet Searles also uses symbiosis in a wider sense and context. Although the actual mother–child symbiosis may be resolved through individuation, the symbiotic mode of existence is never resolved. This is inherent in Searles' idea of the need to constantly re-individuate. It is also true because Searles (1966–7) directly states that the great majority of personality functioning in adults is symbiotic. For all his therapeutic interest in individuation, Searles' (1980) admitted preoccupation with symbiosis must be recalled. Individuation means 'becoming an individual,' and what individuates in people is a sense of having a separate, personal identity. But Searles points out that even the apparently individuated person spends a vast portion of his time in a sort of fused, subliminal connectedness with others and the world at large:

The predominance of personality functioning, even in healthy, adult persons, is subjectively undifferentiated, at an unconscious level at least, from the great inanimate realm of the environment . . . we function in even smaller degree as animate *human* beings . . . we function to a still lesser degree as predominantly *uniquely* living human beings.

(Searles, 1966–7, p. 50)

Most of the time, then, the person simply exists, without awareness, in the world. Just as Searles accepts the inconsistent, pluralistic nature of personal identity, he also seems to accept the fact that people are rarely aware of that identity.

Jung is in agreement with Searles on the fundamentally unconscious quality of human nature. What Searles terms 'symbiosis' seems very close to what Jung (1921, 1931c) calls 'participation mystique.' Jung's concept, which is borrowed from anthropology, denotes a mental state of non-differentiation and identity between a person and the environment. The world exists as total projection (Jung, 1931e). This state of mind is characterized by the animistic world of primitive man, where everything is alive with spirit – trees can talk, and so on. But unless reflexive consciousness intervenes, participation mystique in less severe form – usually between people rather than people and objects – is also the basic mental state of civilized man. As Jung says, it is 'an *a priori* identity of subject and object' (1921, p. 456); in other words, a given. It will be there until consciousness intervenes. And consciousness, notes Jung, 'is a condition which demands a violent effort. You get tired from being conscious. You get exhausted by consciousness. It is an almost unnatural effort' (1935a, p. 10). Hence, consciousness is historically symbolized by the myth of the hero and his daring, lonely deeds (Jung, 1911–12/1952). Jung's viewpoint thus seems similar to Searles' (1966–7) conclusion about the infrequency of even superficial self-awareness.

Although their ideas on individuation are different, it is apparent that the condition a person individuates from is roughly similar in both theories. Both see a basically unconscious condition prevailing in the adult as well as the infant. But Searles stresses particularly the maternal symbiosis, in a fashion that seems incongruent with Jung.

In a curious way, however, Jung also focuses on the mother. As

34

in the matter, cited above, of the 'divine child' and the Self, Jung does so in a symbolic way. For Jung (1911–12/1952, 1944), the entire unconscious is represented by the image of the mother, so a person in a state of 'participation mystique' is, in effect, in the mother. The person without consciousness is a child, psychologically speaking. Jung also describes the unconscious as the 'matrix' (Latin, *mater* = mother) of consciousness (1911–12/1952, p. 219). Consciousness then is born out of the mother-world, the unconscious. This is much like Searles' individuating self separating from the mutually incorporative bond with the actual mother. In addition, in a way that recalls Searles' theory of the alternating states of symbiosis and individuation, the drive for consciousness involves a continual symbolic re-entry into and return from the mother. For Jung this is the true meaning of the incest or 'Oedipus' complex (1911–12/1952, p. 219).

Throughout this discussion of self and individuation, it has appeared that Jung is operating at a more abstract or at least more symbolic level than Searles. It must be remembered, however, that for Jung the 'living symbol' (1921, p. 125) and even 'The Symbolic Life' (1939b) are just that: alive and real. They have the phenomenological, psychic reality upon whose importance both Jung and Searles agree. As later chapters on psychotherapy will show, Searles is also very interested in symbols, particularly symbolic communication between patient and analyst (transference/countertransference) and the repair of damaged, inner imagos or 'objects.' The actual mother–child symbiosis (or lack thereof) is thus raised to a metaphorical level in the analytic relationship.

Finally, at a 'process' level, it is clear that individuation cannot stand alone as a concept. For Searles, it involves continual and even simultaneous interaction with a state of symbiosis. Jung's individuation theory demands ongoing differentiation from a participation mystique created by an infinite unconscious. In both theories, linear concepts of a cause-and-effect or one-time individuation fall before a more complex reality. Individuation is an unclear, cyclical and even paradoxical process. The 'symbiosis → individuation' or 'identity → individuation' paradigms, composed of alternating and sometimes synthesizable polar opposites, are therefore much in keeping with the dialectical assumptions of Searles and Jung.

Summary

This chapter revealed much congruence in Searles' and Jung's basic personality postulates. Fundamental to each of their theories is a potent unconscious, which they define in 'personified' form. Not only the unconscious but the individual's conscious sense of his personality – his 'ego' or sense of 'self' – is a pluralistic phenomenon. Accordingly both authors also stress the preeminent role of awareness of one's diversity.

In their speculations on the origins of personality, Jung and Searles show their first differences. Searles focuses on personal, external, and familial sources, while Jung emphasizes inherited, archetypal structures. Yet both cite the affective basis of the personality, and adhere strongly to evolutionary, phylogenetic developmental concepts.

The mechanisms and dynamics of unconscious processes, particularly introjection and projection, are quite alike in Jung's and Searles' systems. Both theorists also go full circle concerning the 'image vs. reality' conflict in interpersonal relations: projections are false and true. Searles especially notes the reality elements in projections. Paradox, dichotomy and contradiction are fundamental to both men's epistemologies and theories.

The 'inter-subjectivity' that Jung and Searles see at the root of personality formation and interpersonal influence is echoed in the authors' high elevation of subjective reality. But Jung values 'psychic reality' in its own right, while Searles values subjectivity for its accurate perceptions of external reality. Furthermore, while both seek unconscious realities via symbols, Searles looks for the symbolic in personal relationships and Jung in the symbol itself.

Personality and personality growth show up in the authors' theories under the same terms, 'self' and 'individuation.' Jung's 'Self,' however, is more autonomous, more potent, more symbolic and more united than Searles' 'self.' Searles' concepts remain personal and ego-oriented, like his view of the unconscious, whereas Jung's touch on ego-displacing factors. In terms of the process of approaching one's self, 'individuation,' Searles and Jung at first are different, then similar. Searles explains individuation as a childhood endeavor and Jung as an adult one, but then Searles describes it as ongoing and Jung suggests its mediation via birth and child symbols. Both theorists also define individuation as a non-completable process of differentiation through increased consciousness. The authors' differences seem to lie in what is separated from (content) rather than the dynamics of separation (process).

3

PSYCHOPATHOLOGY

Psychopathology, the 'study of diseases of the mind,' can easily take on pejorative or moralistic overtones. It involves assessment, critical judgment and finally a decision about a person's 'mental health.' To categorize a person as 'sick' or, worse, 'crazy' is no small matter – witness the common, derogatory usages of these terms. The consequences of being categorized or seeing oneself as mentally ill are major. A diagnosis itself can change one's life.

The stigma of mental illness – the idea that a person so designated is weird, 'bad' or morally weak – has never been dispelled.[1] And, much like the legal profession, Psychology cannot quite clarify its position *vis-à-vis* personal responsibility for one's pathology. That is, who or what is to blame for this condition?

The traditional, 'medical model' view of psychopathology, which has enjoyed cyclic popularity since pre-Freudian times, is that mental illness is actually physical illness or malfunction in the brain – a 'disease,' like tuberculosis for example, for which a person could probably not be held morally responsible. More psychological or 'dynamic' viewpoints have held periodic sway since Freud invented modern psychotherapy. These would imply, on the surface at least, that a person's mental state is not entirely bound by brain physiology and is therefore under his or her control. However, it is quickly evident that many people who appear 'ill' have neither the intelligence, imagination, nor theatrical ability, much less the inclination, to dream up a full-fledged mental disease, not consciously anyway. Hence, the notion of an unconscious dimension arises.

The influence of the medical-physical point of view on psychopathology extends farther than biochemical hypotheses and responsibility issues. Even though a psychopathologist may deny the biological origins of pathology, he may still tend to look in 'medical' ways at mental illness. He may use medical paradigms and sequences: diagnosis–treatment–prognosis, sickness–health, or 'symptom relief.' A person is treated 'as if' he has a disease, albeit an intangible, mental one.

The 'medical model' might better be called the 'disease model.' It is not inherently right or wrong. Like all models, it simply has its own set of assumptions. Though it is still the predominant view on psychopathology, some of its presuppositions have been challenged in recent years. All forms of challenge rest on the essential questions: is anything really wrong with this individual and, if so, what?

One author (Szasz, 1960, p. 113) suggests that the notion of biochemically diseased, abnormal states is a 'myth.' Such things do not exist. Others look for pathology in families (Bateson *et al.*, 1956) or systems (Minuchin, 1974) rather than an individual's body or mind. Another author (Laing, 1967) hints that psychopathology may be the only sane recourse in an insane society. Returning pathology to the individual, but with a more philosophical orientation, are theorists who point to moral irresponsibility (Mowrer, 1960) or existential dilemmas (May, 1961). In most of these constructions, psychopathology has moved away from the personal disease concept.

Each theory of pathology implies a theory of psychotherapy, and vice versa. Furthermore, since all therapies are approximately equal in effectiveness (Smith *et al.*, 1981), any version of psychopathology may also be appropriate. Presumably they all have heuristic and practical value: one may look for and at pathology in whatever way one chooses.

It is necessary, however, that a theorist be aware of his assumptions, because these assumptions will generally parallel or dictate therapeutic treatment. What a person really thinks about the nature of psychological suffering or sickness is intertwined with his ways of approaching it.

In the preceding chapter, some assumptions about general personality structure and functioning were presented. This chapter will explore Jung's and Searles' views on what has happened to bring the normal personality to grief or to treatment. The focus will be on the nature, sources and meanings of psychopathology as they see it.

Psychopathology?

Chapter 2 revealed that Searles' and Jung's personality theories are, for the most part, derived from clinical practice. Along similar lines, both theorists also believe that accurate generalizations can be made from clients to non-client populations. Both these viewpoints say something about psychopathology. 'Sick/well' or 'us/them' models become immediately obsolete. When the boundaries of illness and health are blurred, normality becomes a relative concept. Abnormality can no longer be lodged 'out there' with intolerably 'different,' strange people. Pathology is possessed to some degree by all – it is truly democratic.

This egalitarian and charitable approach is not unusual for psychotherapists and certainly not exclusive to Jung and Searles. However, just as pathology may be a 'matter of degree,' so is the ability to universalize or empathize with 'abnormality.' Searles and Jung both move toward the more rarified ends of the empathic spectrum.

Searles for instance is fond of quoting Harry Stack Sullivan's (1940) statement to the effect that 'we are all much more simply human than otherwise' (1979, p. 3). As Searles says in his own words:

> Psychosis and sanity are not nearly so *different*, qualitatively, as the patient himself assumes, and as the nonpsychotic part of our population, including psychiatrists who have not worked with these patients, assume.
>
> (Searles, 1976b, p. 596)

In other places, Searles alludes to (1980, p. 26) the psychotic elements in the allegedly 'normal' therapist and decries the therapist's 'unwittingly using the patient to bear the burden of all the severe psychopathology in the whole relationship' (1978, pp. 62–3). In other words, the supposed paragon of normality, the therapist, is also 'ill' in some way.

Whereas Searles implies that all persons have some measure of psychopathology, Jung suggests that an isolated, distinct area called psychopathology does not really exist as such: 'The doctor especially should never lose sight of the fact that diseases are disturbed normal processes and not *entia per se* with a psychology exclusively their own' (1935a, p. 6). Furthermore, from Jung's point of view everyone has 'complexes' – sensitive, inferior or weak areas of the personality that could be called pathological (1905, p. 322). Here, Jung sounds like Searles: pathology is universal. Finally, Jung seems to reject the normative, contextual bases of attributions of psychopathology:

> As long as that man can explain himself to me in such a way that I feel I have contact with him, that man is not crazy. To be crazy is a very relative conception. . . . To be 'crazy' is a social concept, we use social restrictions and definitions in order to distinguish mental disturbances.
>
> (Jung, 1935a, p. 35)

Thus, Searles and Jung both minimize psychopathology as a differential concept: Searles by universalizing it, Jung by questioning its independent existence and validity. Taking different directions, they seem to arrive at a point where 'pathology' is so common or relativized as to lose its original medical meaning. Their shift in outlook involves considering pathology less in the 'disease' sense than in its original etymological sense (simply, from the Greek word *pathologia*, 'the study of the emotions'). The notion of sickness or wellness becomes, for them, secondary to the more empathic notion of 'suffering' (Greek, *pathos*).

To be sure, neither theorist ultimately denies the existence of something that could be defined as psychological illness or psychopathology. Neither is that radical or naïve. But Searles and Jung both shift the context and, more importantly, the approach to psychopathology. They recognize but do not linger on the 'disease' aspect of a problem; instead, it is viewed in a more 'normal' light. Unlike pointless physical illness, mental disease makes a certain kind of sense to them: it is a reasonable phenomenon. Therefore, rather than eliminate psychopathology, they seek to understand its meaning. This is the basis of Jung's statement that certain people owe 'their entire usefulness and reason for existence to a neurosis' (1917, p. 46). Jung's idea that neurosis is not fully cured but is 'outgrown' also reveals his different evaluation of psychopathology (1929b, p. 91). It resembles Searles' standpoint on the 'cure' of psychosis:

> We need to realize that any true sanity, any true mental health, involves the individual's being open to experiencing, at the level of feeling and fantasy and nighttime dreams,

whatever exotic or unconventional psychotic contents had previously overwhelmed the patient.

(Searles, 1976b, pp. 596–7)

From these perspectives, illness is refined and made more manageable. In addition, it is evident that psychopathology marks a possible transition to a new phase of personal development.

Searles, for example, speaks of pathological symptoms as 'transitional objects' in the differentiation of inner/outer reality or object relations (1976a, p. 575). Jung notes the futuristic orientation of illness: 'Hidden in the neurosis is a bit of still undeveloped personality, a precious fragment of the psyche' (1934b, p. 167). This is psychopathology as potential rather than disease. Closely related, of course, is the idea that the cure of pathology will mean the creation of something never before experienced, rather than a return to a pre-illness condition.

Definition

'Normal' personality functions and components outlined in the previous chapter do not automatically delineate areas of psychopathology. That is, abnormality can usually be defined as an alienation from normal processes. However, this does not follow for Searles and Jung because the normal/abnormal boundaries are, in a general sense, blurred. Psychopathology must be viewed in a new light.

While not definable in the usual way as the distortion of standard processes, psychopathology can at least be defined in relation to the personality dynamics the theorists espouse. Each of the personality components and/or issues outlined in the last chapter – the personified unconscious, phylogenetic heritage, unconscious communications, symbiosis and identity, individuation and so on – has particular vicissitudes in the context of pathology. In other words, though Jung and Searles relativize and redefine 'pathology' in many ways, their general formulations about personality take on particular aspects when a person becomes 'ill' and becomes a client or patient.

Their pluralistic approach to personality – personality as a loose composite of distinct complexes or introjects – lends itself to a kind of 'infectious disease' concept of psychological illness. Despite their apparent rejection of the medical model, Jung and

Searles nevertheless employ the medical metaphor with some regularity. Complexes, for instance, become the 'sore spots' in the personality (Jung, 1931a, p. 528); Searles speaks of 'toxic' introjects (1959d, p. 345). It is as if the personality has been bruised, wounded or poisoned by what both authors call 'foreign bodies' (Jung, 1934a, p. 96; Searles, 1958a, p. 213).

Yet, it must be remembered that Jung's complexes and Searles' introjects are judged to be normal phenomena. Therefore, they must be pathological only under certain conditions. Since at other times they are normal, apparently there is a threshold beyond which pathology occurs: it is a matter of degree.

The normality/pathology threshold is highlighted by matters of 'degree' in several senses, actually. For Jung and Searles, the key question is the degree of eclipse of the usual ego functions. Pathology becomes definable when consciousness no longer has consistent control of the personality or the ability to adapt to a situation. In a slightly oversimplified sense, what happens is that one or more of the unconscious personality components or 'selves' overwhelms the previously stable, relatively coordinated sense of identity. Jung describes this as the complex assimilating the ego, such that the usual sense of ego ('I') is modified or even gone (1907, p. 41). In a more colloquial manner, Jung says, 'We are not really masters in our own house' (1935a, p. 73). Searles' (1977a) 'multiple identity processes' refer to a similar absence of conscious control in which assorted, unconscious introjects take turns at the helm of the personality.

However, in both Jung's and Searles' cases, the temporary displacement of conscious, ego-control is not necessarily pathological. Psychopathology is determined less by degree of ego restriction than by the frequency of such shifts in personal identity. A rare instance of what Jung terms 'invasion' (1935a, p. 43) by a complex or Searles calls the 'lively and harmonious interrelatedness' (1977a, p. 462) of internal objects is not a sign of illness. As Jung puts it, 'One can lose one's mind in a more or less normal way' (1935a, p. 24) – for instance, when losing one's temper, falling in love, grieving and so on. But habitual inter-ference or the overly rapid transition between introjects begins to indicate a pathological condition. The introject and its corresponding, often inappropriate behavior pattern may then start to have deleterious effects on self-concept and interpersonal relations. Thus, to have the 'myriad persons' (Searles, 1977a,

p. 462) perpetually in the ascendant is linked to a pathological state.

Another question of degree when assessing illness is the degree of 'foreignness' of the 'foreign bodies' within: how alien or unfamiliar is the constellated introject to the person? A feeling of foreignness (feeling 'funny' or strange to oneself) may be a result of the newness of the introject or its odd, perhaps threatening content. Regardless, that sense of strangeness is a function of lack of understanding by the ego-identity. Stated in still another way, the degree of anxiety-related defensiveness (i.e., lack of conscious awareness) against the complex or object is a measure of pathology. From this perspective, psychopathology is the consequence of a failure to consciously assimilate or integrate the personality. As Searles explains it, the 'innumerable personalities' within exist in an 'undigested' state (1951, p. 60n).

Thus, in terms of the pluralistic personality systems postulated by Searles and Jung, the frequent interference of multiple, inner selves and the failure to understand them is the indicator of psychopathology. Being unpredictable, 'out of control' or even temporarily controlled by introjects is not in itself pathological, but being consistently unconscious of oneself is. This is why Searles, as previously noted, says, 'the more healthy the individual is, the more *consciously* does he live in the *knowledge* that there are myriad "persons" – internal objects each bearing some sense-of-identity value – within him' (1977a, p. 462, italics mine). In fact, according to Searles and Jung, the missing sense of self-control will be alleviated as self-awareness increases.

In some respects the views of Jung and Searles *vis-à-vis* pathology in a multifaceted personality structure seem different. Jung's (1907, 1911) description appears to entail an ego-complex that is already in place, but is later assaulted and gradually overwhelmed by the other complex(es). On the other hand, Searles' view is that a solid sense of personal identity may not have been firmly established in the first place (1961g, p. 524). The core has never been formed. This difference may be a reflection of the fact that Jung seemed to work predominantly with neurotic clients, while Searles' *métier* is schizophrenia.

However, several considerations reveal closer proximity between Jung and Searles than expected. The fact that Jung (1907, 1951a) speaks of the ego as a complex indicates that any sort of indestructible 'core' of personality is not really envisioned in his system. From the beginning, Jung's ego-concept relates more to 'consciousness' (1951a, p. 5) than personality structure as such. Also, if any central, organized core of the personality does exist in Jung's system, it is the Self, which is something to be striven for and is perhaps unachievable (see Chapter 2). Therefore, as with Searles' (1977a) flexible, non-monolithic 'personal identity,' a Jungian concept of personality 'foundations' is already almost a misnomer. Again, it is a question of degree of personality consolidation in both their views.

Furthermore, calling Jung's caseload 'neurotic' and Searles' 'psychotic' may be an oversimplification. Jung notes, though this might be questionable, that it was only after leaving his ten-year practice with hospitalized, chronic psychotics that he 'came into real contact' with schizophrenia, due to the greater proportion of 'latent and potential psychoses' outside the clinic (1958a, p. 258). Many of Jung's clients, with their vivid or hallucinatory experiences of the unconscious, might be diagnosed today as borderline, dissociative or personality disorders. Moreover Searles, once he left hospital practice after fifteen years, began writing with some regularity about 'borderline' patients (Searles, 1969, 1976b, 1976c, 1978, 1986). The discrepancy in diagnostic severity of Jung's and Searles' caseloads may be less than expected.

Finally, regarding the Jung–neurosis, Searles–psychosis question, the unformed core of identity that Searles refers to is distinctly derived from schizophrenic psychopathology. Yet, Jung's 'complex theory' is also a function of his early work with psychotics, about whom he says much the same thing as Searles. Comparing the schizophrenic and the neurotic, Jung theorizes that the schizophrenic

> . . . has the same complexes, the same insights and needs, but not the same certainty with regard to his foundations. Whereas the neurotic can rely instinctively on his personality dissociation never losing its systematic character, so that the unity and inner cohesion of the whole are never seriously jeopardized, the latent schizophrenic must always reckon with the possibility that his very foundations will give way somewhere, that an irretrievable disintegration will set in.
>
> (Jung, 1958a, p. 258)

45

Threats to the fundamental basis of personality suggest a precarious personality structure in the first place, meaning that Jung's above description of the 'latent schizophrenic' has something in common with Searles' outline of the 'pre-schizophrenic' individual (1958b, p. 231). Neither is solid at the core.

Pathological contents

Whether referring to neurosis, character disorder, or psychosis, psychopathology is still a function of the frequency of interference by 'internal selves' combined with the inability to understand those selves. This is how it looks, at any rate, from a theoretical, structural point of view. Some of Searles' and Jung's most vivid studies describe psychopathology from the less abstract, phenomenological perspective of the client himself, the 'sick' person who is apparently suffering.

In this context it is the content of the introjects and complexes that is important, because the pathological structural dynamics that are set in motion are an effect rather than a cause of the multiple persons within. The nature of the content is what keeps it 'undigested' by the client: it is what makes the 'foreign bodies' foreign.

In terms of psychopathology, the chief component of interest in an introject or complex is emotion. Although Searles and Jung devote much theoretical effort to the formation and etiology of internal images, the heart of the issue, from the client's point of view, is the *feeling* quality. This is why Jung often refers to complexes as 'the feeling-toned complexes' (1907, p. 40; 1934a, p. 93). The 'nucleus' or core of a complex – what gives it its power and what initially creates it – is its 'feeling tone' or 'intensity of affect' (Jung, 1928b, pp. 11–12). Though interrelated, images and mental associations are somewhat secondary to emotion.

Searles' early work likewise greatly emphasizes emotion over personality structures, the latter being conceived of as ego-defenses against feeling. And even after modifying his position to correlate affective and structural realms, Searles still stresses the emotional qualities of the introjects and introjected situations upon which identity is built (1965b, pp. 27–8). Jung seems to sum up both theorists' positions when he says, 'The essential basis of our personality is affectivity. Thought and action are, as it were, only symptoms of affectivity' (1907, p. 38).

Feelings, of course, must always be about something. And the context and direction of emotion-charged contents is slightly different for Searles than Jung. Searles' reference point is almost exclusively the parents and family, at least as far as psychopathology is concerned. In terms of chronology, the feelings are ones that have existed since childhood, though they are embodied in an ongoing, living introject in the present day as well. Jung also suggests that pathogenic complexes are frequently associated with the immediate family, but he is not so exclusive about this as Searles, nor does he restrict the time element to the early, infantile years. According to Jung, the complex is simply a highly emotional 'image of a certain psychic situation' (1934a, p. 96), usually connected to an upsetting 'personal matter' (1911, p. 598) of past, recent or continuing importance. Often this does relate to parents or others, but there may also be a more generalized, situational determinant, as in a money- or power-complex.

The kinds of feelings that may be encapsulated in an introject are as varied as the emotions themselves. Most often the feeling is disturbing to the client. In the context particularly of a client's parents, Searles repeatedly points out feelings of grief, nostalgia, jealousy, disloyalty, rage, rejection and criticism, to name but a few. Jung is less detailed but notes that the feeling-tone of a complex is almost always 'painful' (1934a, p. 99).

Yet both authors also discover on occasion what are usually considered to be more appropriate or positive emotions amongst the multiple selves in the unconscious. Furthermore, they sometimes ascribe crucial pathogenic import to them. For example, Searles mentions feelings of love, adoration and genuine solicitude that often lie beneath the previously cited negative aspects of an introject (1958b, p. 216). Actually, what tends to occur is that positive emotions exist in conjunction with negative emotions. Often the latter are caused by the former, as when a painful feeling of guilt results from the sincere, loving, but unsuccessful desire to 'cure' one's disturbed parents (Searles, 1966a, 1975a). Jung generally categorizes the feeling-toned complexes under the somewhat ominous heading of the 'shadow' – the repressed, inferior, unsocialized aspect of the personality (1951a, p. 8). But Jung also suggests that under certain circumstances the shadow may contain most of a person's more positive aspects. Someone's 'moral side' (Jung, 1917, p. 20) may exist in the shadow-complex, not to mention 'a number of good qualities, such as normal instincts, appropriate reactions, realistic insights, creative impulses, etc.' (Jung, 1951a, p. 266).

Several things become clear from this discussion of pathological content. First, Searles delineates the ambivalence of the introject – the simultaneous or causative interaction of its emotional components – more precisely than Jung does. Jung merely gives an overview of possible emotions and general contexts, whereas Searles specifies emotions and a context (the family). Second, it is evident that the content of internal objects is neither predetermined nor inherently positive or negative. Nor is it simple. In Jung's and Searles' theories, an introject or complex is not a single, discrete impulse of a theoretically preordained nature (e.g., a repressed psychosexual desire for a parent). Rather, the content consists of a whole web of complicated feelings about a particular person or situation. The pathological aspect of an introject lies less in the situation itself, however traumatic, than in the client's conflicts about or failure to react fully to that situation. This leads to a third consideration about content. It is not simply feelings that reside unintegrated in a complex. Also lodged in the introject are realizations about the problem or oneself. Naturally, such cognitive understandings are usually intermingled with strong emotions, or may cause distasteful emotions when realized. Still, the principal, core content of an internal object can be an unrealized realization as well as an unrealized emotion. Searles cites, for instance, the psychopathological significance of a client's inability to realize that his parents see him not as he is but as narcissistic, fantasized extensions of themselves (1964, p. 722). As above, Jung speaks of 'realistic insights' embodied in the unconscious complex (1951a, p. 266).

Defenses

If, as Jung and Searles postulate, the emotional content of introjects is sometimes positive, sometimes insightful, and not specified *a priori*, the question that arises is: What then makes the inner selves 'indigestible'? After all, it is the client's failure at assimilation of content that is the keynote of psychopathology, not the content itself. In addition, the failure to consciously integrate introjects exacerbates them. They tend to interfere more frequently in proportion to the client's inability to understand them – a sort of vicious cycle of increasing unconscious pressure coupled with an increasingly confused, weakening consciousness.

The question then is really one of defense. The emotional content of the introject(s), whether actually positive or negative, is assumed by the client to be something negative. 'Assumed' is not the correct word – it is felt to be somehow threatening. Therefore, it is kept indigestible, unassimilated, pathological.

Defenses make introjects indigestible, but Searles' and Jung's views on defense show variation. Searles' emphasis is on the repressed or denied introject and its contents – on the avoided. Although defenses are unconscious mechanisms, they play an extremely active role in his theory of psychopathology. Searles lists not only standard psychoanalytic fare (denial, repression, projection, intellectualization, etc.) but includes symptomatic mental states like confusion, perplexity, uncertainty, vengefulness and even delusions amongst defense mechanisms (Searles, 1952, 1956). Normal introjective processes like identification and incorporation, cited in Chapter 2, can also be used defensively to avoid intolerable affect (Searles, 1951, 1967a). What many theorists see as products of a so-called disease, Searles sees as the disease. Indeed, almost the whole symptomology and experience of schizophrenia, which Searles describes psychodynamically as 'ego fragmentation and ego dedifferentiation' (1967a, p. 16), is considered an unconscious defense against intense, ambivalent emotions. Defenses are the disease.

Jung's posture on defenses is much less developed and less emphasized than Searles'. The mechanism Jung mentions most often is repression, using this in the sense of an active, almost conscious denial of 'incompatible' (1920, p. 310) tendencies associated with the 'shadow.' Jung may really mean 'suppression' here. Like Searles, Jung also can interpret certain activities normally considered symptomatic (e.g., homosexuality) as defenses against more intense emotions (1917, p. 87). And Jung mentions a kind of chronic defensiveness that results from the continuous build-up of pressure from unrealized complexes – in other words, a defensive character structure (1921, p. 279).

But Jung's theory of the unconscious is such that a detailed description of defense mechanisms is not necessary. In Jung's view, the unconscious is composed less of 'incompatible' emotional tendencies that must be repressed than it is of contents that have simply lost their energy or of spontaneously emerging contents that have never before been in evidence (1920, 1951a). Difficulties in assimilation – a key factor in pathology – are not necessarily the result of defensive maneuvers. Rather, the client is 'not yet' capable of understanding the new contents embodied in the complex.

Jung's (1936a) hypothesis of an impersonal 'collective unconscious' lends itself to this distinction between the defensively avoided and the not yet understood. The irrupting contents from the unconscious may be 'archetypes,' whose strangeness, power and impersonality make them initially incomprehensible. These 'internal selves' do not have a personal reference point or history against which the client might be defending. The heavy emotional overtone of this type of complex is not a function of defensive operations in Searles' sense; it is inherent in the archetypal experience itself.

If defenses do arise, according to Jung they will most likely be reactions to 'the objective, inner activity of the psyche' or the 'inner voice' (1934d, p. 183). Resistance to integrating such spiritual/archetypal dimensions of experience as Jung postulates might well be considered natural rather than defensive in the usual sense. In effect, the client is being asked to assimilate not just distasteful personal emotions but transpersonal, collective contents. For Jung, the archetypes are, literally, 'the gods' (1936a, p. 23). Adding these 'psychic factors' to one's personal identity can require a change in *Weltanschauung* and self-concept a good deal more radical than 'owning,' for example, one's long-repressed ambivalence toward a parent.

In a certain, general sense, Searles and Jung share the similarity that they both create new 'defenses' to fit their viewpoints. Just as Searles (1952) adds an important array of functional mechanisms (perplexity, uncertainty, etc.) to traditional analytic theory, Jung outlines a number of possible reactions to the onslaught of the collective unconscious. What Jung calls 'negative attempts to free the individuality from the collective psyche' (1928a, p. 163) are actually defenses against the potentially shattering effects on consciousness of archetypal contents. Among these Jungian defenses are: 1) 'regressive restoration of the persona' – a denial of the archetypal experience and a defensive return to an earlier, narrower personality level; and 2) 'identification with the collective psyche' – a self-inflated, cultish attitude of possessing unique spiritual wisdom (Jung, 1928a, pp. 163, 169).

Thus, both Jung and Searles develop new concepts about defenses against autonomous complexes. But they are really speaking about different levels of defense. Searles refers to resistances to disturbing personal emotions, whereas Jung alludes to escapes from nonpersonal, sometimes spiritual matters. In addition, Searles' generally negative opinions about mysticism suggest that Jung's theory of the collective unconscious might itself be an immature defense[2] against painful 'Good Mother/Bad Mother' emotional experiences on the personal level (Searles, 1960, pp. 107–8).[3] However, the 'infantile omnipotence' (Searles, 1960) that Searles attributes to such archetypal states sounds parallel to the kind of megalomania that Jung frowns on as 'identification' with the collective unconscious.

Clearly, both authors are anti-omnipotence. In terms of defense, as elsewhere, their real difference lies in the transcendental factors Jung ascribes to the unconscious. Although each theorist develops new aspects of the 'defense' issue, Searles invents new defenses whereas Jung invents new contexts for defenses.

Origins

The dynamic sources of psychopathology have been hinted at or directly stated in much of the preceding description. Painful or conflictual events give rise to defensively unassimilated emotional reactions, which take the form of pathogenic introjects. The dynamic context of such events is, for Searles, the immediate family and, for Jung, any highly affective, personal or impersonal relationship.

In psychological terms, however, the traumatic 'event' that leads to psychopathology only rarely is a discrete happenstance. More accurately, a psychological event is a series of interactions, an ongoing relationship, with a characteristic set of diverse emotions. Thus, a 'mother complex' (Jung, 1954d, p. 85) or an 'early mother introject' (Searles, 1964, p. 719) is not derived from a single event, however abusive or depriving, but from a whole fabric or gestalt of interactions.

Jung, more so than Searles, admits the possibility in his early work of a sudden trauma engendering a complex: 'There are impressions which last a lifetime' (1907, p. 43). But the example Jung gives is taken from legend. Even the 'spontaneous' irruption into the personality of the historical archetypes, an internal process which Jung (1939a, p. 287) posits as a potential cause of mental illness, has a slowly developing 'incubation' period in the unconscious (1920, p. 307). Likewise, Searles makes no mention of solitary incidents that cause pathological introjects. Childhood as a whole is the incident that leads to illness.

If the cause of pathology is a psychological event (defined in the 'ongoing' sense, as above) combined with assorted integrative/defensive factors, the origin may be looked at in a slightly different way. In other words, what makes one ill, dynamically speaking, may be separated from where it begins. The precipitating factor or 'starting point' of the illness is what is meant here by the 'origin.'

The question of origins brings up a wider issue of context that has heretofore only been hinted at. So far, psychopathology has mostly been seen from the client's perspective. It has at least been implied, however, that the emotional core of pathogenic introjects must relate to something or someone. In Searles' case this means parents and, in Jung's, personal and impersonal figures. But taking the client's vantage point tends to create the impression that the emotional forces embodied in introjects originate in the client and move outward toward significant others. Likewise, focusing on 'defense' parameters tends to center the discussion on what the client is doing (repressing, denying, identifying, etc.). Thus all the emotional vectors are either isolated within the client or thrusting 'out' into the world.

But, when they widen their fields of view to incorporate the acute emotional effects of other people on the client, Searles and Jung soon begin to approach a 'systems' theory of psycho-pathology. While emphasizing the ultimate responsibility of the client himself for maintaining or changing his predicament and pathology (a treatment issue), Searles and Jung each suggest, though to different extents, that the source of illness may be people in the client's environment.

They mean this quite literally. They do not mean that the divisive effects of others have confused or crippled the client, who then becomes ill. They mean that the psychological disturbance exists and originates in another person. The disturbance then transfers to the client in full or near-complete form.

The mechanisms of transfer are the unconscious communication processes – identification, incorporation, introjection/projection, intuition – that are postulated by Jung and Searles (see Chapter 2).

52

Just as the foundations of the emerging personality are formed by complex introjective processes, so one's identity may be misformed by them. In terms of pathological origins, the question of 'where?' now becomes the question of 'who?' And the 'who' most frequently spoken of is the parents.

Searles particularly focuses on the pathological effects that ill parents have on offspring via mutual introjective processes. While he does not categorically state that the parents of the future schizophrenic are themselves psychotic (though he does offer many examples of just that), he cites repeated instances of baffling, chilling parental behavior vis-à-vis the child (Searles, 1958a, 1961d, 1964, 1967a). Such behaviors are almost certainly pathological, often forming part of an unconscious 'effort to drive the other person crazy' (Searles, 1959a, p. 254). As Searles sees it, parent and child can then become involved in a competitive struggle to see who will become insane, with the winner usually being the parent.

The 'craziness' that is bandied about in this situation would have to originate in the parents. Nowhere in Searles' writing is there evidence of a genetic or 'constitutional' theory that would imply the child's being born insane. In fact, if there is something that is 'innate' in children, according to Searles it would be a universal 'psychotherapeutic striving' toward others, especially the parents (1975a, p. 380). As with the attempt to drive other persons crazy, such therapeutic efforts by children are largely unconscious. Yet they remain for Searles the major etiological factor in psychopathology.

In practice, what makes this therapeutic striving so pathogenic is that the pre-psychotic child (later the schizophrenic adolescent or adult) relinquishes his emerging ego-identity, his individuation, in favor of becoming a 'symbiotic therapist' to the ill parents, particularly the 'ego-fragmented' mother (Searles, 1975a, pp. 338, 385). Returning to the question of 'whose pathology?', Searles summarizes all of the above in this way:

> He [the child] sacrifices his potential individuality in a dedicated effort to preserve her [the mother's] precarious integration through introjecting the dissociated components of her personality, components which become distortedly personified, and in a sense crystallized, in the schizophrenic illness.
>
> (Searles, 1961a, p. 349)

Earlier, it was stated that 'defense is the disease.' From the current perspective it appears that the mother is the disease, or at least the origin of disease. In effect, the mother has succeeded in unconsciously externalizing upon her child her own craziness (Searles, 1959a, p. 265). The child meanwhile identifies with her pathological model and furthermore tries to cure the mother – for both their sakes – by incorporating her pathogenic introjects, anxieties, sense of worthlessness, sense of being 'nonhuman,' and so on. Both parent and child thus exist in a symbiotic, pre-individuation state. Neither is a whole person. Together they form a dependent, pathological 'whole,' cemented together ambivalently by defensive combinations of loyalty, love, guilt and threat – a case of the whole being less than the sum of its parts.

Lest it appear that the mother is the sole source of pathology, Searles implicates the father, the husband–wife relationship, and the 'family' system as well. 'Narcissistic,' 'autistic' or 'depressed' fathers, among many others, are introjected by future clients, just as mothers are (Searles, 1967a, pp. 6–7; 1969, p. 118). Not only are the individual behaviors of parents fragmenting to the child, but the parents' relationship to each other may be grossly disturbed and integrated as such by the child (Searles, 1959d, p. 323). If a person's sense of identity is built on internalization of the parents, this means, according to Searles, that the client may have to introject two totally discordant people (1967a, p. 5).[4] The discrepancy in identification makes for perceptual and emotional confusion, not to mention conflict.

The whole family also plays a role in perpetuating as well as engendering such pathogenic introjections. Searles notes that the future client becomes the implicit 'spokesman' for the pathological intra- or interpersonal relations of the entire family (1967a, p. 11). Yet if he expresses or otherwise enacts a consciousness of this role or these family traits, the client may be called 'crazy' by the family. Thus awareness itself is considered pathological, and the child's trust in his own perceptions is doubly bound and undermined. He receives no verification of his tentative feelings and ideas. Similarly, efforts at individuation by the child come to be sensed as a threat to the interlocking 'family symbiosis' of non-individuated parents and siblings (Searles, 1964, p. 733). Because personal identity is symbiotically bound to family identity, separation from the family is tantamount to loss of identity.

Although he expands the potential sources of a client's psychopathology to include others besides the mother, Searles nevertheless devotes most of his attention to her pathology. If anyone besides the client himself is to 'blame' for the illness, it is she. But in discussing these maternal origins of illness, Searles widens the field still further to include not just the mother but the mother's mother. In effect, Searles (1958b, 1961a) is postulating an ancestral source of psychopathology, transferred from generation to generation and lodged in the present-day client.

Specifically, as a result of her symbiotic relationship with *her own* mother, the patient's mother suffers from very low self-esteem and a consequent repression of her loving feelings toward her own child, the future client (Searles, 1958b, p. 224). She cannot accept the child's love and adoration of her.[5]

This causes the child, in turn, to feel a worthlessness and malevolence similar to what the mother feels – it is thus a result of what the mother herself felt as a child. The child's sense of minimal self-esteem comes from his identity with his mother's past and from her rejection of him in the present.

While he does not talk in detail about the grandmother's pathology, Searles does suggest that the current pathological symbiosis is a function of 'a transference to the child, on the mother's part, of feelings and attitudes originally operative in a symbiotic relationship which obtained between herself as a small child and her own mother' (1958b, p. 225).

Furthermore, to make this multigenerational transmission of pathology even more complicated, Searles (1975a) hypothesizes that the mother projects her own mother-introject (the grandmother imago) onto the child. Thus the child is reacted to in projection not only as the mother's repressed and hopeless 'child-self,' but as the mother's own rejecting or omnipotent mother. Since the mother never blamed the grandmother for rejecting or psychologically abandoning her, the mother can now blame the transference-mother embodied in the child. Thus the accused client feels more than ever like the 'unwanted child' due to ancestral sources (Searles, 1975a, 1976c).

Where it all begins (or ends) is never fully tackled by Searles or Jung, nor could it be. Jung too puts great credence in the ancestral sources of mental illness. He does this in a number of ways, some of which are very consistent with Searles, some very different.

Whereas Searles talks about the future effects in adulthood of parental disturbances, Jung speaks of parental effects with direct reference to psychopathology in childhood. This may be another way of saying that Jung writes about child psychopathology, while Searles seems to only feature adolescent or adult. At any rate, Jung's categorical statement on pathology in children is not only that it comes from the parents but that it is frequently the parents' own illness(es) (1926, p. 69; 1931g, p. 43). Again, this transfer of illness takes place via the mechanism of participation mystique, a preexisting, unconscious identity between child and parents (see Chapter 2). Jung does not speculate on any positive or negative motivations involved in this condition of mutuality. He presents no Searles-like findings of unconscious therapeutic strivings or attempts to drive others insane. But even though he does not interpret the facts, Jung's facts sound very much like Searles':

> In early infancy the psyche is to a large extent part of the maternal psyche, and will soon become part of the paternal psyche as well. The prime psychological condition is one of fusion with the psychology of the parents.
>
> (Jung, 1928d, p. 53)

Jung continues with reference to pathology: 'All parental difficulties reflect themselves without fail in the psyche of the child, sometimes with pathological results' (Jung, 1928d, p. 53).

Parental difficulties may take on individual or collective form, though the two are often intermingled. Jung's examples show repressed complexes in either the mother or father about sexuality, intellectual development, social ambitions and even religious issues. Criminality, laziness, low-life inclinations and other unconscious shadow qualities of 'successful' parents may be embodied in an errant offspring (Jung, 1931g, p. 43) – a sort of 'karmic' debt for the overly gleaming personae and lifestyle of the parents.

General dissatisfactions between the parents, that is, their relationship, also permeate the atmosphere and can infect the child. As Jung explains:

> The child is helplessly exposed to the psychic influence of the parents and is bound to copy their self-deception, their insincerity, hypocrisy, cowardice, self-righteousness, and selfish regard for their own comfort.
>
> (Jung, 1926, p. 79)

In this regard, again, it must be remembered that, for Jung as with Searles, this 'psychic influence' is unconscious in all participants (Jung, 1928d, p. 55).

By and large Jung pays less attention than Searles to siblings and the immediate family as a whole system. Jung emphasizes child and parents. Yet he does make at least one 'systems' statement of interest:

> We are constantly coming up against the experience that in a family of several children only one of them will react to the unconscious of the parents with a marked degree of identity, while the others show no such reaction.
>
> (Jung, 1931g, p. 42)

This hints at Searles' remark about the isolated client being locked into the role of 'spokesman' for the 'dissociated personality traits' of the family (1967a, p. 11).

Like Searles, Jung ultimately returns to the mother as the chief if not the only source of childhood problems. Jung is less direct but the focus is clear: 'Whenever a young child exhibits the symptoms of neurosis ... one should begin one's investigation elsewhere, starting with the mother' (1926, p. 69). And just as Searles notes the multiple projections of mother onto child, including 'nonhuman' part-selves, Jung is highly critical of a whole class of pathogenic mothers who ambitiously treat their children as 'things' rather than people: 'The children of such mothers are practically nothing more than dolls to be dressed up and adorned at pleasure ... nothing but mute figures on a chessboard' (1926, p. 127). Searles' book on the *Nonhuman Environment* cites actual examples of schizophrenic patients who subjectively experience themselves as precisely such things as dolls, and were treated as such by their parents (1960, p. 216).

Jung's summarizing statements about the nature of the pathologies that are transferred from parent to child fall under the general category of what he calls 'unlived life' (1921, p. 183). Children are psychologically compelled to fill in the gaps in their parents' existence. Jung means specifically 'that part of their [parents'] lives which *might have been* lived,' only it was repressed or avoided (1931g, p. 43). According to Jung, children unconsciously seem obligated to compensate and repair this moral failure by 'acting out,' in both senses of the phrase, these positive or negative, 'unlived' aspects.

This concept of Jung's sounds suspiciously like Searles' of 'therapeutic strivings' on the part of children toward parents (1975a, p. 382). However, Searles interprets the child's activity as a loving attempt to help the mother become whole, so she then can be a successful mother and model to the child. In contrast, Jung's interpretation again centers on a sense of the child's compensation as a sort of 'destiny,' without distinctly therapeutic or even very personalized attributes. Still, he does seem generally sympathetic to the plight of such a child, and even mentions a case where he analyzed a client's 'erotic and religious problem' through the dreams of this client's young son (Jung, 1928d, p. 53). The son was dreaming for the father – a sort of 'acting in' rather than living out that Searles, at least, might see as therapeutic (even if ambivalently symbiotic).

Though it appears at first that Jung places the source of child pathology exclusively in the mother or parents, Jung moves to an 'ancestral' viewpoint that is very much like Searles'. When speaking of 'unlived life,' Jung ultimately wonders 'how much of the blame really rests with the parents.' He mentions the 'ancestors' and the concept of 'original sin,' then warns that the parents are themselves 'children of the grandparents' (1931g, p. 43). His conclusion is that, via psychic infection mediated by participation mystique, 'neurotic states are often passed on from generation to generation, like the curse of Atreus' (Jung, 1926, p. 78). Thus the origins of illness may lie farther back in time. By the same token, Jung also speculates that the source of the child's healthy individuality may also lie with 'the grandparents and the great-grandparents, who are the true progenitors' (1931g, p. 44). Hereditary transmissions can therefore be positive or negative.

So far, a subtle but crucial distinction between Jung and Searles has been that Searles stresses ancestral effects on the child that influence his becoming an ill adult. Jung's emphasis has been on pathology in children, although this context naturally overlaps with adolescents and adults to some degree. Yet as Jung's opus develops over time, extending deeper and deeper into a theory of a collective unconscious, psychopathology becomes increasingly related to the realm of the ancestors, but in a rather different sense than when Jung discusses children. The issue of inheritance becomes an issue of impersonal transmissions rather than personal ones. What are inherited are virtually timeless personality facets, the archetypes, rather than time-bound family introjects. The transmission process does not involve external family inputs; rather, the primordial, collective unconscious, which forms 'the true basis of the individual psyche' (Jung, 1931b, p. 152), is simply born again in every child (Jung, 1954c, p. 66). This is an internal transference, from one generation to another, dependent on genetics and not on generational causality.

As noted earlier in the discussion on complexes, adult psychopathology for Jung is essentially a matter of the client's relationship to these archetypal complexes. When neglected, the mythological systems mediated by archetypes explode and overtake consciousness, making archetypes 'the unfailing causes of neurotic and even psychotic disorders' (Jung, 1941, p. 157). Whereas in children the family appears to be the source of illness, in adults it is the 'ancestors' in the more general sense of one's prehistoric relatives, one's 'archaic' inheritance. Along these lines, Jung seems to emphasize the 'personal' complexes (of the parents) in children, but the archetypal complexes (of the collective unconscious) in adults.

If ancestral inheritance in adult pathology means for Jung something impersonal and internally oriented, then it seems Jung has gone to the other end of the spectrum from Searles' external, family-derived transmissions. However, in a paradoxical way Jung's archetypal complexes involve the outer more than the isolated individual's 'inner' world.

Jung's concept of the collective unconscious actually has such comprehensive dimensions that it takes in the outer world and social contexts as well as the internal realm. Aside from the fact that all personalities have a common, collective basis in Jung's theory, the collective unconscious also moves individuals simultaneously and *en masse*. In other words, similar archetypes may be constellated in many people at the same time. Jung describes the phenomenon in this way:

> When the archetypes are activated in a number of individuals and come to the surface, we are in the midst of history . . . The archetypal image which the moment requires gets into life, and everybody is seized by it.
>
> (Jung, 1935a, p. 103)

Thus the archetypes are sort of historical, collective vectors that nevertheless may manifest themselves in the individual. They are potent, transcendental forces shaping current events and society, insofar as society is an aggregate of individuals so affected. This is the ultimate 'systems' theory – where each individual in an entire society, not just a particular family, can be moved by underlying factors that affect the system as a whole. The scale of the ancestral inheritance in Jung's theory is literally timeless and worldwide.

On a smaller scale too – for Jung's focus is constantly shifting – archetypes may relate to a particular individual's own needs and concerns. Although certain people seem to be especially sensitive to the unconscious, collective issues of the age (Jung, 1920, p. 314), some clients are struggling with personal disturbances in their own 'inner or outer adaptation' (Jung, 1916b, p. 449). Faced with an insoluble, external problem, an archetypal image may arise from the collective unconscious to re-orient and enlighten (Jung, 1954b, p. 21). In terms of inner needs, a disconnection from the archetypal roots of personality, such that an individual is separated from a sense of 'mankind' or the world of 'spirit' (Jung, 1929a, p. 320), may result in irruptions or possession by the ignored autonomous archetypes. According to Jung, the archetypes, formerly the 'gods,' can then reappear as phobias, compulsions and other symptoms (1929b, p. 113). Or, pathology aside, the spontaneous manifestation of numinous, archetypal experience may represent the 'initiation process' into the mysteries of the self – 'individuation' (Jung, 1953a, p. 523). Thus, collective events of the time may affect an individual, or an individual may be victim (or recipient) of collective compensations for personal needs, external or religious.

So, returning to pathology *per se*, world-shaking forces, perhaps connected to the overall psychological needs of the age or *Zeitgeist*, may arise in one individual or many individuals. As Jung says, 'Our personal psychology is just a thin skin, a ripple on the ocean of collective psychology' (1935a, p. 163). On a similarly grand scale, archetypes may be constellated in reaction to or in conjunction with outer, sociopolitical events. Social situations may reactivate eternal archetypes, sometimes even resulting in a 'mass psychosis' of the sort Jung attributed to Germany under Nazism (1948c, p. 607). Whether personal or impersonal internal movements or sociocultural externals come first, Jung's fundamental point is that 'Private life, private aetiologies, and private neuroses have become almost a fiction in the world of today' (1936a, p. 48). Jung thus skips right past Searles' hypothesized source of adult illness, the family, and into the family of man as origin.

Regression/progression

As Searles and Jung extend their theories of psychopathology by reconstructing the time and social dimensions involved, the two theorists also begin to reorient their notions of the inherent qualities of illness. The general nature of this change of perspective was discussed at the beginning of this chapter. Searles and Jung see pathology less as disease process than as a transitional phase, purposeful compensation (Searles, 1967a, p. 15; Jung, 1917, pp. 110–11) or attempt at healthy change. The attempt at growth may not be successful, but the spirit of the pathology is not necessarily so bad. At its worst, the pathology presents a relentless challenge or demand to the client; at best, it has a purpose. The challenge is to find out that purpose. For Searles and Jung, pathology is potential.

The earlier discussion of the 'ancestral' offered a number of examples of purposiveness at the heart of pathology. Searles' description of a child's 'therapeutic striving' toward a sick parent, resulting in the sacrifice of self in order to be a 'symbiotic therapist,' is clearly an act not only of love but of unconscious purpose. Though the effort fails, the goal is appropriate: to help the parents grow up so they can help the child grow up. The illness is the pathological symbiosis, but that symbiosis is an attempt at self-cure. Likewise, Jung's basic interpretation of any neurosis is, 'An act of adaptation that has failed' (1913, p. 250). In addition, Jung's archetypal complexes, though they resemble the outbreak of psychosis, may be forceful compensations for the problems of the individual or the time he lives in, or harbingers of the individuation process. Although Jung's scope is larger than Searles', the goal of pathology in their theories is similarly non-pathological and future-oriented.

This linkage of the ancestral and the teleological comes together for both in their theories of regression. Regression is commonly considered a pathological phenomenon, a retreat to a less adaptive, infantile state. Most analytic literature therefore classifies it as a defense mechanism. Both Jung and Searles, however, see regression not as defensive, but as something that is defended against. Instead of alleviating anxiety, regressive maneuvers in fact tend to create anxiety.

The reason why regression is not anxiety-binding is that it is connected with 'phylogenetic inheritance' (see Chapter 2). Just as infantile development retraces phylogenetic stages, adult regression follows the same steps, only backwards. The regressing client is in some danger of devolving into his prehuman, ancestral roots. In Searles' theory this can mean regression to an inanimate, 'nonhuman' level (1960, p. 250). Jung calls this the 'preconscious, prenatal phase' (1911–12/1952, p. 181). Regressive movements may stop, of course, anywhere along the way, but when Searles and Jung speak of regression they are usually referring to a full-scale 'phylogenetic regression.'

That such a psychological movement is anxiety-producing seems self-evident. What Searles terms 'the devastating loss of adult functions' (1960, p. 179) is certainly frightening in itself, especially if it means returning subjectively to 'an animal, vegetable or even inorganic state' (p. 130). An aspect of this anxiety that both authors mention is the fear not just of regressing to prehuman states, but of staying there. What Searles would seem to describe, literally, as becoming a vegetable, Jung speaks of more generally as the threat of 'dissolution and extinction in the unconscious' (1911–12/1952, p. 354) – in other words, death, or a death-in-life. Related to this is the fear of insanity, and Jung (1911–12/1952) and Searles (1960) both derive their theories of 'phylogenetic regression' from work with schizophrenic patients. Furthermore, both frequently describe insanity in terms of regression. Searles (1960, p. 146) defines psychosis as a regression into primitive modes of experiencing, a state he calls 'dedifferentiation' (of outer and inner, fantasy and reality, I and you, etc.). Jung is less direct, but does call schizophrenia a 'regression to archetypes' (1936b, p. 570n).

So far, phylogenetic regression looks only like a rather disastrous, pathological 'dissolution' or 'dedifferentiation' of personal identity. At this point, though, Jung and Searles both bring in its teleological aspect and interpret the phenomenon in positive terms. Searles criticizes the standard, 'defensive-substitute' definition of regression because it does not 'go far enough' – not far enough in a number of ways (1960, p. 251). First, literally, most theories do not envision the possibility of dedifferentiation to subjectively prehuman levels. Second, and more important, classic analytic theory forgets people's 'ceaseless striving (whether at a conscious or unconscious level) toward further psychological growth, toward further emotional maturation' (Searles, 1960, p. 251). Regression, for Searles, is part of that ceaseless striving.

Jung's view and even his criticisms are similar, as evidenced by the fact that his massive work (1911–12/1952) on the purposive, transformative aspects of regressing 'libido' led to his departure from the psychoanalytic movement and Freud. In general, Jung notes that what 'at first sight looks like an alarming regression is rather a *reculer pour mieux sauter*, an amassing and integration of powers that will develop into a new order' (1935b, pp. 15–16).

How regression comes to be 'restitutive' (Searles) or 'recuperative' (Jung) is explained by the theorists in parallel fashion. Searles sees the backwards movement of functioning and perception as an effort to get a fresh start on the emotional problems at hand (1960, p. 251). The client regresses to some earlier state, wherever he can find it, of comfort or solidity. Sometimes this state may resemble an inanimate one. The individual is unconsciously searching for a pre-stress condition, from which he can gain enough security to return and adapt to the present situation. Although this purposive aspect is difficult to see while it is happening, particularly when the client is engaged in highly regressed behaviors, Searles concludes that 'regression can be seen, in retrospect, as a phase of the recovery process – a phase of emergence of what is youngest and healthiest in the patient' (1960, p. 252). Searles adds that some of his long-psychotic clients even look physically younger, and symbolic products like dreams seem to monitor their progress with images of healthy, new pets or young children. He also describes one catatonic client's achievement of 'rebirth' through phylogenetic regression (p. 258).

This emphasis on youth, rebirth and symbolic imagery is the highlight of Jung's explanation of regression, even more so than Searles'. In fact, whereas Searles focuses chiefly on the person who is regressing, Jung centers on the regressive nature of the person's fantasies. This distinction allows Jung to outline in more detail the hows and whys of the regression process. He ties regression to introversion, incest, symbol formation and the transformation of psychic energy. Overall, however, the goal of regression is the same for Jung as for Searles: 'rebirth' (Jung, 1911–12/1952, p. 224).

In Jung's theory the process of phylogenetic regression begins in the same place as Searles', namely, 'at moments when a new orientation and new adaptation are necessary' (Jung, 1911–12/1952, p. 293). Unable to cope with a new problem, the progressive movement of psychic energy or 'libido' comes to a halt. The energy flows backwards into the unconscious (regression, introversion) with a corresponding devaluation of the outer, real world (Jung, 1928b, p. 33). This retreat from reality seems to invoke symbols and fantasies linked with the mother; therefore, it has forbidden, incestuous connotations. So, while Searles (1960, p. 180) believes that regression produces anxiety lest one become nonhuman, Jung (1911–12/1952, p. 213) seems to suggest that the resistance is due to fear of incest. Despite this apparent difference in explanation, Searles does define the goal of this process as 'a chronologically earlier relatedness' providing 'satisfaction, security and peace' (1960, p. 251). From Jung's perspective, these latter characteristics can be symbolized by the mother (1954d, p. 82).

At any rate, this apparently incestuous goal is not to be taken literally, according to Jung. The meaning of the regression is not physical incest but 'the strange idea of becoming a child again, of returning to the parental shelter, and of entering into the mother in order to be reborn through her' (Jung, 1911–12/1952, pp. 223–4). This again echoes the earlier, protected state postulated by Searles.

The aforementioned incest taboo ultimately has little to do with resistance in Jung's opinion. What it does do is rechannel regressing libido into other symbolic directions, constellating the potentially helpful archetypes related to the adaptive problem (Jung, 1911–12/1952, pp. 293–4). The rebirth that occurs is not through the mother as such, but through the unconscious, which is symbolized by the mother.

Thus, the movement and function of phylogenetic regression is quite similar in both men's theories. A chaotic step backwards permits a forward step. Searles envisages a sort of oasis at the end of the regression, at which one can re-charge and move out again. The corresponding development in Jung's version is finding the archetypal content that may contain 'a revelation, or a saving idea' (Jung, 1911–12/1952). In both instances, something is found in regression that may lead to progression and adaptation.

Certain differences in emphasis exist between Searles and Jung, some of which have already been hinted at. Searles is primarily interested in regressive behavior, but Jung refers to regressive imaginal activity. Similarly, Searles centers on persons and Jung on energy transformations. Because Jung hypothesizes a collective unconscious, he can specify the actual dynamics of regressive process more fully than Searles. He places it in the context of libido theory and the archetypes, while Searles speaks of schizophrenia, only in general. Searles does not outline the means to the positive ends of regression.

However, these shades of difference are minor. Even the apparent distinctions, such as persons vs. fantasies, fade on closer inspection. For instance, Searles' notion of psychosis as regression to a dedifferentiated state means that the behavior of the schizophrenic is itself very symbolic. With no inner/outer boundaries and a minimal level of ego-consciousness, the schizo- phrenic is to some extent a sort of walking 'unconscious.' He is in a continuous fantasy. One could even say he is a fantasy. From Jung's perspective, such a person would be acting out the collective unconscious. In fact, Jung actually says this: 'In schizophrenics ... the collective contents of the unconscious predominate strongly in the form of mythological motifs' (1951, p. 483). Thus Jung and Searles are both dealing with regressive fantasies, even if in Searles' examples the person does not realize it is fantasy.

Diagnosis

In the final analysis, Jung and Searles return psychopathology to the patient. Deviating from the medical model view that psychopathology is necessarily 'pathology,' an alien disease, they instead ascribe a twin aspect to it. It is disease and potential. They emphasize the latter, perhaps because treatment is more important to them than a formal, academic nosology. As the above discussions of the 'ancestral,' in all facets, and regression respectively show, pathology offers meaning (historical) and direction (future) to the pathologized person.

The two theorists also return pathology to the client in the sense that they often let it speak for itself. This takes the form of approaching the pathology from the point of view of the client. Although they may interpret the client's subjective experience of the world or his fantasy life psychodynamically, Searles and Jung also give full weight to the experiences as they are. Searles goes to great lengths to understand the 'schizophrenic individual's experience of his world' (1967a, p. 5). Jung was the first psychologist to show that the utterances of psychotics have discernible meaning (1907).

Their phenomenological approach to pathology even extends to the ways they categorize it. In Jung's theory, standard diagnostic considerations have a secondary, *ex post facto* place:

> Diagnosis is a highly irrelevant affair since, apart from sticking a more or less lucky label to a neurotic condition, nothing is gained by it, least of all as regards prognosis and therapy. . . . It [the diagnosis] manifests itself only in the course of treatment. Hence the paradox that the true psychological diagnosis becomes apparent only at the end.
>
> (Jung, 1945, pp. 86–7)

Jung then proceeds to replace the usual diagnostic criteria with non-medical categories based on the client's experience, particularly his unconscious experience: shadow, anima/animus, Self. Jung tends to diagnose, then, in terms of the autonomous complexes and archetypes.

Searles has less overt criticism to offer about diagnosis *per se*, though he does condemn almost any contrivance, including diagnosis, that may serve to defend the therapist against emotional involvement with a client (Searles, 1977d, pp. 285–6). Like Jung, Searles develops idiosyncratic diagnostic criteria, but he does not focus on introjects to the same extent as Jung. Rather, Searles (1961g) assesses the relationship between therapist and client, who will be lodged in: autism, ambivalent (pathological) symbiosis, preambivalent (therapeutic) symbiosis, or individuation. While Jung categorizes complexes, Searles diagnoses the quality of the therapist/client interaction. But by definition, because it depends on issues in therapy, Searles' method resembles Jung's above statement that the diagnosis 'manifests itself only in the course of treatment.' Thus, both theorists use the standard definitions initially, but, when it comes to therapy itself, they diagnose in a manner closer to their theoretical underpinnings.

The final word on psychopathology here harks back to some of the perspectives on pathology keynoted in this chapter: the client's viewpoint, adaptive failure, energy considerations, neurosis vs. psychosis. This last word belongs to Searles, but it is the one place in his entire work where he quotes Jung. Searles comments on Jung's statement that ' "a peculiar psychic inertia, hostile to change and progress, is the fundamental condition of neurosis" .... This is, as we know, even more true of psychosis' (1961d, p. 447). Thus Jung and Searles come together on psychopathology.

Summary

Highlighting Searles' and Jung's views on psychopathology is their parallel opinion that mental illness is not really illness. Each author stresses its transitional and even positive aspects. In 'phylogenetic regression' this becomes particularly clear, and there is distinct correspondence in their theories and examples. The only divergence is that Searles postulates a deeper potential regression (nonhuman); Jung's archetypal perspective, however, is much more comprehensive concerning archaic psychological states.

When approaching pathology as an entity rather than a healing process, Jung and Searles show much congruence. An over-frequent displacement of the person's sense of identity by his 'selves' helps define psychopathology. Both authors also mention the client's failure to meet this internal challenge with self-awareness. Weakness of consciousness, then, is inherent in most pathology and, in schizophrenia, Jung and Searles suggest an overall weakness of the personality.

Though secondary in defining pathology *per se*, the contents of pathological states are important to both patients and therapists. According to Searles and Jung, contents are emotionally painful but positive, multidimensional and often cognitive. Nevertheless, the writers' differing views of the unconscious color their perspectives: Searles is more detailed on personal emotions, while Jung spends less time on the 'shadow' than on the archetypal. Their theories on defense show the same differences, accordingly. Yet both men develop original ideas about defense mechanisms.

Aside from structural difficulties in the individual, Jung and Searles both place the roots of pathology in the patient's family and 'past.' For Searles this holds true for all clients. For Jung the family is a source of illness in children only, while in adults the relationship to a distant, archetypal past demands attention.

Ancestrally speaking, Searles and Jung coincide only as far as the personal forebears. In terms of origins, Jung's space and time coordinates are much wider than Searles'.

Finally, both theorists return pathology to the client in his own terms and for his own benefit. The individual's subjective experience guides both authors' understandings of the pathology, just as it guides the client (often teleologically). Jung and Searles quickly forego standard diagnosis in favor of diagnostic explanations that correspond to patient and treatment realities.

4

THE PROCESS OF PSYCHOTHERAPY

The process of psychotherapy – how therapy 'proceeds' – is a virtually all-encompassing topic, and certainly the central one in any discussion of psychotherapy. More than simply describing the stages of therapy, this chapter will discuss in some detail what journalism calls the 'Five W's': who, what, where, when and why. It will also consider 'how' therapy works: the dynamics of cure as postulated by Jung and Searles.

The usual sequence of events used when explaining the therapy process will be reversed in this chapter. The 'goals' of the process are presented first. Then the chapter pursues the core aspects of psychotherapy: 'transference/countertransference' and 'working with the unconscious.' Finally an overview, the 'stages' of therapy, is outlined. The 'dynamics of cure' question runs through the entire chapter, but receives special attention in the middle, core sections, especially in the 'transference' section.

In its non-linear fashion this chapter resembles therapy itself. It starts with some idea of the goals to be reached. Then the heart of the process is entered into. At the end, one attempts to describe, in orderly fashion and in retrospect, what has happened.

Goals

The process of psychotherapy has to do with a sequence of psychological moments between therapist and client, an engagement that somehow results in cure, change or something that may be called an amelioration of psychopathology. It is perhaps not out of place to explicate what that amelioration really consists of. Working backwards then, the end-point or goals of the treatment process merit attention first.

Many of the aims of therapy have been indirectly or directly stated in earlier chapters. Pathology, defined as an influx of introjects combined with lack of awareness, is 'cured' by means of awareness (an awareness which grows out of an emotional relationship with the analyst). As consciousness increases, pathology lessens. In addition, the pathogenic introjects inherent in pathology change simultaneously with awareness. That is, as the orbiting complexes come closer to consciousness, they lose their alien, disturbing effect. Jung puts it this way: 'The unconscious is not rigid – it reflects the face we turn towards it' (1944, p. 25). In other words, the attitude of the ego and the degree of awareness can have positive or negative effects on the complexes (the components of the unconscious). As the conscious attitude toward the 'inner selves' becomes more accepting, they become more acceptable.

Another way of stating this goal, increased consciousness, is in terms of the withdrawal of projections. Through the therapy process, the introjects that a person experiences 'out there' in the world are experienced as subjective aspects of the personality. This makes the world less burdened by unconscious, sometimes falsifying, 'imagos.' Reality then has the opportunity to be seen more closely as it is. The goal of awareness or projection–withdrawal, then, has two facets: it means consciousness and change of one's inner self(ves), and it means a more accurate perception of people and the external world, too.

But things are not so simple. The withdrawal of projections through the re-integration of imagos is a matter of degree, as is the degree of actual change in the introjects themselves. First, as noted in Chapter 2, there is always contamination between object and inner imago, and this interplay is not necessarily misguided. Searles calls this overlap the 'nuclei of reality' in projected contents (1975b, p. 374); Jung calls it the projection 'hook' (1946, p. 191). This 'reality' factor means that the integration of introjects is not a simple matter of delusion vs. clarity, with external reality suddenly beaming forth in its 'objective' essence. Second, assimilation is an ongoing process because projection never ends, even in the 'normal' adult (Searles, 1961e, p. 474; Jung, 1951a, p. 20). This is especially true with Jung's system, with its hypotheses of a limitless, generative unconscious and its stress on the world, even the world of sense perceptions, as a psychic world of 'carefully processed images' (1933, p. 384). Third, Searles' definition of 'healthy identity' as 'myriad internal objects functioning in lively and harmonious interrelatedness' suggests that it is not so much the 'myriad persons' but the individual's awareness that changes as a result of therapy (1977a, p. 462). Similarly, there are Jungian complexes, especially the impersonal ones (anima, animus, Self), that cannot really be incorporated into the ego's personal inventory without causing psychopathology (Jung, 1928a, 1950a, 1951a). While archetypal contents can be assimilated, the archetypes themselves cannot be (Jung, 1951a, p. 20). Therefore, such selves, and the unconscious as a whole, can only be befriended in a continuing way, much as Searles prescribes relating to one's 'multiple identity.'

If projection–withdrawal is an imperfect process, with personality components being not so much changed as cleaned up and brought home to the 'ego family,' it would seem that both theorists' notions of cure are relativized. The goal of the therapy process ceases to be reversal of pathology *per se*. The aim is now awareness and, through awareness, repair of the inner imagos.

This sort of growth, of course, is the goal of treatment from the therapist's viewpoint. As such, it is a 'process' goal, defined in terms closer to the therapy situation itself than, for instance, an external goal of a better marriage, symptom relief or job satisfaction. These latter criteria might be the client's goals, at least originally. However, Searles and Jung do discuss therapy's aims from the client's less technical perspective. Searles comments on 'realizable goals' for the client as follows:

> One needs to come to reject, for example, the goal of enduring freedom from envy, or guilt, or whatnot . . . . One does not become free from feelings in the course of maturation or in the course of becoming well during psychoanalysis; one becomes, instead, increasingly free to experience feelings of all sorts.
>
> (Searles, 1966a, pp. 34–5)

This is a less structured, client-centered way of saying what Searles says more formally about multiple-identity functioning.

'Feelings' are what are embodied in the technical term, 'imagos.' Jung could be speaking to and for a client when he similarly states:

> My aim is to bring about a psychic state in which my patient

71

begins to experiment with his own nature – a state of fluidity, change, and growth where nothing is externally fixed and hopelessly petrified.

(Jung, 1931f, p. 46)

Elsewhere, Jung also seems to echo Searles' emphasis on 'feelings of all sorts' (including painful):

... the principal aim of psychotherapy is not to transport the patient to an impossible state of happiness, but to help him acquire steadfastness and philosophic patience in face of suffering. Life demands for its completion and fulfillment a balance between joy and sorrow.

(Jung, 1943a, p. 81)

This viewpoint, too, gives deeper experience and change of attitude preference over changes or removal of the complex *per se*.

At this point, psychotherapy looks like an 'awareness' process, a kind of healthy narcissism, whose goal is not making pathogenic introjects disappear or 'not hurt,' but making them tolerable through awareness. While the inner selves do not 'go away,' and do not change, perhaps, as much as might be wished, this is not to imply that they are not transformed at all. Searles (1977a) and Jung (1934a) stress the normality of an introject-dominated, pluralistic self, yet they also emphasize what could be called the 'symbolic repair' of introjects. That is, the pathological imagos comprising the patient's identity need to be detoxified in some way during the treatment process.

For instance, Searles, who stresses the pathogenic importance of the mother and mother-imago (see Chapter 3), suggests that therapy might achieve for the patient:

... an internalized *image* of her [the mother] as being, however many-sided in her identity, essentially whole and a fit keystone, therefore, for his own sense of identity. . . . [T]he whole treatment consists in an attempt to help the (internalized) parent to achieve a whole, integrated identity.

(Searles, 1966–7, p. 57)

Though he attributes less pathological potential to the actual parents than to the neglected archetypes, Jung (1928a, 1951a) also proposes an ongoing refinement and purification of the imagos in the unconscious and the contents that the imagos, in effect, produce (1934a, p. 101). He speaks through alchemical imagery of therapy as a process in which the 'superfluities' belonging to the complex are purified (the alchemists' 'mundificatio') or, in analytic terms, worked through (Jung, 1946, p. 277). Similarly, the central archetype of the Self is approached through the increasing refinement of symbols: individuation is a process 'in images and of images' (Jung, 1954b, p. 38).

In Jung's case, this process seems to be less a matter of symbol-repair than of elucidating and amplifying unconscious complexes that are simply 'not yet' conscious (Jung, 1951a, p. 4). These complexes are not repressed but lie in waiting. Searles' attention lies in actually 'fixing' the image of the pathogenic parent which the client has introjected. Even so, a chief component of Searles' repair is not just re-experiencing repressed emotions but experiencing them, in a manner of speaking, for the first time (1978, p. 47). Searles' introjects, then, can have a 'not yet' aspect similar to Jung's complexes.

Ultimately, it is neither clear nor particularly important whether the introject is an 'old' one or a 'new' one, or whether some imagos need repair while others need to be discovered. The goal of therapy remains more functional, less debilitating introjects, and more accessible awareness of them.

There are other therapy goals, of course, that both analysts delineate. Searles points to 'continuity of identity' as an aim (1961g, p. 554). He means, referring to schizophrenic patients, that the successful client experiences his pre-psychotic past, his psychotic present and his non-psychotic future as connected aspects of himself. Among other things, this is really a space-time consideration: the client is no longer unhooked in time or 'lost in space,' but has an ongoing sense of personal reality. This, too, is close to Jung's definition of the ego: 'You have a certain idea of having been a long series of memories' (1935a, p. 11). So Searles is really suggesting a goal of continuous ego-identity.

Jung cites even more general goals, such as 'wholeness' (1943b, p. 819) and 'self-knowledge' (1955–6, p. 474). He lists elsewhere a whole raft of 'typical and temporary terminations' that in many cases can signal an end of therapy if not an achievement of ultimate aims (Jung, 1944, p. 4). Among these are better adaptations, symptom relief, and meaningful insights, to name but a few.

However, these other goals postulated by Jung and Searles all rest on the fundamental 'process' goal discussed earlier in this chapter – the repair and understanding of the introjects is the basis of the more broadly defined achievements of 'identity' or 'wholeness.' Symbol-repair is the actual or 'micro' form of the larger, abstract goals. Besides, approaching treatment goals at the smaller level permits linkage with the therapy process itself.

For it is evident that the goals of therapy are directly tied to the process of therapy. If the goal is, for example, to resuscitate the damaged, 'internalized' parent, then the process of therapy incorporates precisely that. But not only are aims mixed with process. Given the just-described ways that Jung and Searles define therapy's goals, it is also evident that the process goes on after therapy, that in a certain sense therapy never ends. Literally it does end, of course (though some treatments might well be termed 'endless'; see Searles, 1980, and Jung, 1961a). But the 'spirit' of therapy, or perhaps what is learned in therapy, has continuous application, even after termination. As Jung points out, 'Adaptation is never achieved once and for all' (1916a, p. 73). Accordingly, Searles and Jung both implicitly sanction a quasi-therapeutic attitude toward future difficulties – the client will solve problems as if he were still in therapy. The 'graduate' of therapy approaches later issues with the same style (of awareness, non-repression, fantasy, or whatever) that he evolved in the therapy process.

The dynamics of this learning process possibly may involve the client's internalization during treatment of the 'participant-observer' abilities (Searles, 1977c, p. 581) or the 'healing factors' (Jung, 1945, p. 88) that are present (hopefully) in the therapist's personality. A tacit goal (or result) of therapy, then, may be to develop or internalize a kind of 'therapist imago' or 'inner analyst.'[1] Even if it is not true that therapy lasts forever, it may at least be true that the client takes the 'therapist' with him when he goes.

Transference/countertransference

The goal of treatment is an improved relationship with one's unconscious selves and, as it turns out, the way to get there is also through relationship. For Jung and Searles, it is the relationship between therapist and client that is the fundamental factor and mode of cure. This does not mean simply that the participants have a 'professional' relationship in which the therapist offers good advice or interpretations. Rather, it is the emotional interaction between client and doctor that is the basis of treatment. Therapy becomes a very deep relationship between two people, a matter of intimacy rather than professional distance (or, better stated, a matter of intimacy within a professional context).

Searles characterizes the process of psychotherapy in general as 'an evolutionary sequence of specific, and very deep, feeling-involvements in which the therapist as well as the client becomes caught up' (1961g, p. 521). His emphasis here and throughout his writings is on the depth and mutuality of the relationship. Similarly, Jung describes therapy as the 'reciprocal reaction of two psychic systems' (1935b, p. 4) and adds that the therapist's 'genuine participation, going right beyond professional routine, is absolutely imperative' (Jung, 1946, p. 199).

The interaction, then, is intensely experienced by each participant. Given the 'unconscious communications' postulated by both theorists, such personal involvement between analyst and client is in fact unavoidable. In historical context, this conclusion is of great importance because it represents a parallel divergence on Jung's and Searles' parts from the 'detached' stance espoused by classically Freudian and many nonanalytic therapies. Not only is the emotional influence of patient on therapist inevitable, but both theorists hint that attempts to avoid involvement by clinging to 'neutrality' are morally reprehensible, dishonest or even unethical (Jung, 1946, p. 171; Searles, 1976b, p. 587).

Besides being intense, the emotional engagement between client and analyst also turns out to be larger than both of them. According to Jung and Searles, the process, once undertaken, controls the participants rather than vice versa. Even for the therapist, therapy is often something he joins rather than guides (as Searles says above, the analyst is 'caught up'). Already, a 'leaderless' process has been postulated in terms of the unconscious purposiveness of 'phylogenetic regression' (see Chapter 3). Likewise, in terms of the analytic interaction, Searles states that doctor and patient are 'in the grips of a process, the therapeutic process,' which is

> ... far too powerful for either the patient or himself [the therapist] to be able at all to deflect it, consciously and willfully and singlehandedly, away from the confluent

channel which it is tending – with irresistible power, if we can give ourselves up to the current – to form for itself.

(Searles, 1961g, p. 559)

Jung uses similar terms to suggest that therapy cannot really be grasped, but holds one 'in its grip' (1946, p. 322). Therefore, he prayerfully invokes the greater powers: the therapist is effective and therapy works 'Deo concedente' – God willing (p. 190). In a way this resembles Searles' reliance on faith and trust ('if we can give ourselves up to the current').

However, the degree and type of affective participation that ensues between client and therapist is only hinted at by mention of the analyst's own active participation and the autonomous power of the process. The actual nature of their involvement is far more complicated and difficult. For what occurs during therapy is a potentially chaotic mixing of the two personalities. Searles and Jung mean this almost concretely, or at least as concretely as it can be taken in the psychological domain.

Jung uses scientific analogies to describe the 'chemistry' of the interaction: 'This bond is often of such intensity that we could almost speak of a "combination." When two chemical substances combine, both are altered' (1946, p. 171). Later he states, 'Psychological induction inevitably causes the two parties to get involved . . . and to be themselves transformed in the process' (p. 199).

This degree of intermingling of personalities, to the extent that both are profoundly changed, is repeatedly discussed by Searles (1961g) under the rubric of 'symbiosis,' which can be either 'therapeutic' or 'pathological.' In either form of symbiosis, the interaction is one of 'subjective oneness . . . with a lack of felt ego-boundaries between the two participants' (Searles, 1959d, p. 339). Besides the earlier quoted analogy with a river ('confluence,' 'current'), Searles compares symbiotic relatedness to a 'merry-go-round' (1961g, p. 543). This centrifugal movement in therapy results in a 're-creation of the patient's world . . . but a new world is created for the therapist, too, out of such deeply symbiotic experience' (Searles, 1963a, pp. 643–4). Searles really means that the client does not change alone. Transformation of the analyst in fact is so crucial that Searles feels that the therapist must reluctantly realize that

> . . . the patient cannot totally 'cure' him – that he [the therapist] will have to struggle towards increasing maturity,

increasing personal integration and differentiation, in future courses of work with the patients who will succeed this one.

(Searles, 1961g, p. 548)

This highly affective and mutually transformative 'bond' of therapist and client has a specific, technical name: transference.[2] And from a 'technical' point of view, what occurs when personalities mix is that the multiple selves belonging to each person are mutually introjected. As noted in Chapter 2, the precise means of such transfers are 'unconscious' (unknown), but they do somehow happen through the unconscious: ego-boundaries and psychological separation grow weaker at the underlying 'symbiotic' or 'collective' levels of reality that Searles and Jung postulate.

An additional aspect of transference is projection. According to Jung (1946), when projections are withdrawn from their original 'hooks' (most often the parents), the imagos then lodge in the therapist. This is when transference 'begins.' If this sounds like a phenomenon that occurs only during therapy, Jung clarifies by saying that transference is present in any intimate relationship and, in terms of the analyst, 'It is often in full swing before he has even opened his mouth' (1946, p. 171). This point of view is in line with Searles', whose almost total attention from the beginning of treatment is on the transference.

Searles in fact does not even consider preliminary, pre-transference steps like Jung's (1929c, p. 61) 'confession' or 'elucidation' of personal problems. Nor does Searles delve much into sources of cure other than the transference relationship, though this may have more to do with the nature of his caseload than with his orientation. Unlike Searles, Jung treated clients on a short-term basis as well as long-term. Therefore, Jung can cite instances where transference becomes somewhat secondary and 'the patient's insight plays an important part, also his goodwill, the doctor's authority, suggestion, good advice, understanding, sympathy, encouragement, etc.' (1946, p. 173). Jung adds, however, 'Naturally the more serious cases do not come into this category.'

Still, Jung (1935a, p. 152; 1946, p. 164) on occasion expresses some sincere doubt about the absolute necessity of transference, whereas Searles says:

Unlike psychotherapy as I have usually heard or read of it, wherein patient and therapist explore together what is going

77

on in the patient's life outside the office, my focus is primarily upon what transpires in the office – upon the analysis of transference.

(Searles, 1976b, p. 584)

But this apparent difference of degree may be a function not only of the long-term/short-term distinction but of: 1) Jung's perhaps reactionary stance toward the Freudian demand that transference must always occur, usually in sexual form, or 2) Jung's resistance to the massive 'claims' (1946, p. 173) transference places on the therapist. Here, Searles (1976a) actually has very similar reservations, only his reaction to traditional Freudianism is that it does not go far enough into the transference realities for the therapist as well as the patient (i.e., countertransference). He comments, like Jung, on the 'full agony of the subjective incompetence, impotence, and malevolence' he feels in his work (Searles, 1976b, pp. 583–4). And he casually notes that often 'the patient's illness is causing more suffering to the therapist than the patient' (Searles, 1967b, p. 73). Jung seems to suffer similar agonies: 'Difficult cases are a veritable ordeal' (1951b, p. 116).

At any rate, despite his reservations about this trying phenomenon, Jung's (1946) definitive paper on transference stresses that virtually all serious cases revolve around it and that successful treatment depends on it. His final conclusion is that transference is the 'crux, or at any rate the crucial experience, in any thorough-going analysis' (Jung, 1958c, p. vii). Thus he ultimately joins Searles in highlighting the central position of the transference.

These technical matters aside, it becomes clear that Searles and Jung propose a very specific type of mixing of personalities, one that turns out to be entirely appropriate to the healing process. Although transference in a general sense may be a total combination of projections, introjects, and personalities, both theorists narrow its focus to a therapeutic intermingling of the 'well' and the 'ill' elements in the persons involved. Specifically, it is a matter of the therapist's mental health mixing with the client's psychopathology. Searles describes this interchange as follows:

The therapist, at the deepest levels of the therapeutic interaction, temporarily introjects the patient's pathogenic conflicts, and deals with them at an intrapsychic,

78

unconscious as well as conscious, level, bringing to bear upon them the capacities of his own relatively strong ego.

(Searles, 1958a, p. 214)

Jung says in like fashion that the analyst 'quite literally takes over the sufferings of his patient and shares them with him' (1946, p. 172). As for the therapist's superior state of health, Jung also parallels Searles: 'We must suppose as a matter of course that the doctor is the better able to make the constellated contents conscious' (1946, p. 176). Later Jung adds that the 'doctor's knowledge, like a flickering lamp, is the one dim light in the darkness' (1946, p. 197).

This parallel view of transference in Jung's and Searles' theories does more than define the nature of the interaction. It also explains some of the dynamics of the 'cure.' 'Transference' really means a transfer of the *illness* itself from client to therapist. For Jung and Searles, this is no abstract concept nor a manner of speaking – it is the crux of the 'feeling involvement' or 'chemical reaction' between the therapy participants. For the therapist, therapy often means a real 'psychic infection' (Jung, 1946, p. 177) or 'counter-transference psychosis' (Searles, 1978, p. 51). The therapist now has the illness.

This quasi-literal 'transference' does not imply that the client is cured, having unloaded the disease. It is perhaps more accurate to say that the therapist now has the illness, too. Or the pathology may exist, during more constructive moments, in a neutral or third 'place' in which therapist and client are both actively at work on it. Regardless, the pathology becomes truly mutual; and this may be the real reason why Searles and Jung, respectively, call the transference 'agony' or 'ordeal' for the analyst.

Indeed, the implication by both theorists that the therapist voluntarily takes on the emotional illness of the client may be a rather gratuitous misconception. Given the power and universality of 'unconscious communications,' the therapist probably could not avoid the illness anyway. The only voluntary thing about transference is the therapist's initial decision to get involved. After that, there is no escape, or shouldn't be, according to Searles and Jung.

The two theorists implicitly acknowledge this 'involuntary' element in the following ways. Jung adopts a fateful or fatalistic attitude:

The doctor knows – or at least he should know – that he did not choose this career by chance ... psychic infections, however superfluous they seem to him, are in fact the predestined concomitants of his work, and this is fully in accord with the instinctive disposition of his own life.

(Jung, 1946, p. 177)

Searles also offers evidence that the participation of the therapist is involuntary. He sometimes vicariously experiences clients' physical pathologies (Searles, 1970a, 1976a) or finds clients 'disturbingly present' within himself (1971, p. 135). He also mentions his more psychological sensing that he is at times literally the client's 'illness' (1961g, p. 533). This latter phenomenon is common enough that Searles sees it as indicative of a standard phase of the therapy process, the 'ambivalent symbiosis' (1961g, p. 533). Jung, incidentally, also cites cases of 'psychotic intervals' and 'induced paranoia' in certain therapists, though he does not include himself (1946, p. 172).

A key component in the process of psychotherapy, then, is the infectious transfer of the sickness to the therapist, who is better equipped emotionally to deal with it. For therapy to succeed, the client must 'use' the therapist in this way, and the latter must permit himself to be so used. It appears that, for Jung and Searles, therapy is effective to the exact extent that the therapist allows himself to be affected (or infected) by the patient.

The cure dynamic in the transference involves the therapist's working over the illness or ill personality of the client, then returning it to him, as it were. Searles outlines this process in technical detail, explaining that all the client's pathogenic introjects must be re-projected or transferred over to the therapist (1976a). After 'intrapsychic therapeutic work' is performed by the therapist, the client then re-introjects the now less pathological selves (Searles, 1958a, p. 214). In a slightly more inclusive manner, Searles also describes this process in terms of the client's multiple 'self-images' being gradually united in the therapist's single image of the client (1967a, p. 24). That is, the therapist integrates each facet of the client and a coherent 'feeling-image' of the client is formed in the therapist. According to Searles the client may then proceed to 'identify' with this new, more complete 'self' (1967a, 1967b).

Jung describes a similar dynamic of change, though with

different shades of emphasis. He is less concerned about the specific pathogenic introjects being transferred to the therapist, in part because the inner selves Jung is interested in are often archetypal rather than personal or parental. Instead Jung theorizes that contents of the collective unconscious are activated in the client, and transferred to the therapist, where they 'constellate the corresponding unconscious material [in the therapist] . . . owing to the inductive effect which always emanates from projections' (1946, p. 176). Thus Jung does not suggest, like Searles (1976a, p. 532), that 'all the figures from the patient's own past' must be seen in the therapist. Nor does Jung say as directly as Searles that the therapist consciously and unconsciously works over the introjects before returning them to the client. Again, the 'impersonal' nature of Jungian introjects means that they are only to a minimal extent composed of personal, repressed elements (images, feelings) that could be owned or re-owned as such by the client. Their archetypal quality means these complexes will always be a bit alien and transcendent, 'objective' rather than subjective. Instead, Jung's view of the 'repair' involves therapist and client mutually working through and amplifying the archetypal content that now underlies *both* of them. The transformation here involves a 'symbolic' experience, whereby the impersonal imagos are delineated. Analyst and patient become engaged in the 'transformation of the third' (Jung, 1946, p. 199) – the 'third' being the symbolic synthesis of the conflict in the personality.

This Jungian notion of a union via symbols (individuation) places the dynamic emphasis somewhat beyond the actual transference relationship, which now seems to be the support or ground rather than the direct focus of treatment. In Searles' theory, the relationship between client and therapist is always the center of the transformation.

Overall then, whereas for Searles the synthesis of the client's fragmented personality first occurs in another person (the analyst), for Jung it is mediated by symbols. Because it happens in the therapist, Searles must postulate a re-introjection or identification by the client with the wholeness seen in the therapist. Jung's theory does not need this step: the remediation theoretically is happening already via the symbol. Furthermore, this is the only way it can occur in Jung's system, because the unified 'third' thing is by nature transcendent. It can only be suggested by an image approximating the unknown reality.

This latter distinction harks back to the earlier discussion (see Chapter 2) of the differences between Searles' 'self' and Jung's 'Self.' For epistemological reasons, Jung's Self cannot be fully realized (Jung, 1928a, p. 177). It is a greater, spiritual personality. Therefore, what is 'introjected' in Jung's final transference step is the 'anima' function – i.e., a relationship to 'the higher world of the spirit' (1946, pp. 229–30). For Searles, only the new, 'three-dimensional' self-image is internalized (1967a, p. 24).

It appears that Searles and Jung part company on this 'symbolic vs. interpersonal' dynamic of cure via transference. However, in both instances the re-integration of the personality, whether it be in terms of self-image (Searles) or image of the Self (Jung), happens outside the client. In Jung's case, it actually happens in the collective unconscious, which can only be known symbolically and is not really a personal possession of the client. Hence it is, in a manner of speaking, 'outside' – though it is an internal world. Searles' synthesis is literally 'over there' in the therapist. Yet it is worthwhile to note that the projections and introjections that play such a crucial role at the beginning and end of Searlesian transference are all mediated by unconscious processes. If Searles' cure does not happen 'in' the unconscious, important transfers – from 'sick' client to 'well' therapist and then back again to make a 'well' client – are certainly effected through the unconscious.

Returning now from cure dynamics to 'process' considerations, there is further similarity in the ways Searles and Jung describe the means to these synthetic ends of transference. An assumption made by both theorists (see above) is that the therapist's mental health is superior to the pathologized client's. Therefore it is easy to assume that all the health lies with the therapist and all the illness with the client. Searles and Jung come essentially to a more moderate position in which, as above, the therapist already possesses more adaptive and better articulated ego-functions. However, this is not to say that the therapist has no pathology. The fact, for instance, that both authors speak of 'hooks' and 'reality nuclei' for all projected contents applies equally well to the client's projection of illness onto the therapist: there must be some 'sickness' reality there for the client to hang his projection on.

But both authors go beyond the 'projection' element. Searles believes it is not only unknowing but untherapeutic for the therapist to allow the client to 'bear the burden of all the severe pathology in the whole relationship' (1978, p. 63). That is, much illness is rightfully the therapist's. Jung also suggests that the therapist's normality 'in a deeper sense is an open question' (1946, pp. 176–7). Moreover (and crucially), according to Jung it is the therapist's 'own hurt that gives the measure of his power to heal' (1951b, p. 116).

Therefore, just as 'health' is a relative conception for Jung and Searles (see Chapter 3), so is the issue of 'illness.' The analyst's pathology is not simply the result of transference: it exists in itself.

Beyond the interesting ramifications of the therapist having his own reservoirs of psychopathology, it becomes evident that, without the therapist's 'illness,' therapy simply would not work (at least not in the way that Jung and Searles describe). Why? Because the therapist's pathology enables the transference to occur, and the transference in turn facilitates the cure. Jung implies this when he says above that the therapist's own wounds lend him the 'power to heal.' Searles is even more explicit:

> The more ill a patient is, the more does his successful treatment require that he become, and be implicitly acknowledged as having become, a therapist to his officially designated therapist, the analyst.
>
> (Searles, 1975a, p. 381)

This viewpoint, which Searles calls 'nothing less than a metamorphosis' in the theory of analytic cure (p. 384), also means 'nothing less' than that the therapist is really 'sick' and the client must cure him, at least to some extent. What enables the client's cure to happen is the fact of the therapist's pre-existing pathology. This pathology in the analyst, incidentally, tends to dovetail with the pathology of the client's parents (an inference being that the therapist has a pretty wide range of available pathology). The idea of 'The Patient as Therapist to his Analyst' (Searles, 1975a) also corrects the client's early attempts and failures to be a 'symbiotic therapist' to those pathogenic parents (see Chapter 3). Thus, another part of the dynamic of cure is the client's successful curing of the transference-parents in the form of the analyst.

Even though the above sounds like a cure in projection, the avenue for all this is the reality of the therapist's own illness (which corresponds to the 'reality nuclei' in the client's projections). While it is possible to separate the reality of therapist pathology from the client's projection in terms of degree, it is not possible to do so in terms of quality (Searles, 1949/79). In terms of treatment Searles basically recommends that, regardless of the difference in degree, the important thing is that the therapist be changed, whether his illness is exaggerated by the client or not. So whereas Jung says the therapist's illness gives the therapist 'the power to heal,' Searles is saying that it gives the client the power to heal the therapist and thereby heal himself (the client).

But change in the therapist is not really done by the client and certainly not consciously, at least not in the same way as the therapist therapeutizes the client. Searles does not mean that the doctor brings his problems to the sessions for the client to work on, interpret, etc. It must be remembered that, despite the fact that Jung and especially Searles attribute heavy pathology to the therapist, they also attribute a higher level of consciousness to him than to the client. The changes that are postulated to occur in the analyst are really achieved by the therapist himself. The client provides the impetus, but the therapist provides the understanding. He does the work himself.

What this means in terms of the 'process' of therapy is that the therapist as well as the client is really 'in therapy.' It was suggested in the 'Goals' section of this chapter that, for the client, 'therapy never ends.' Now the same thing appears to be true for the therapist, who 'is as much in the analysis as the patient' (Jung, 1929c, p. 72). And Jung does not mean that the therapist was once in analysis himself but that he is in analysis now with the client:

> The analyst must go on learning endlessly. . . . A good half
> of every treatment that probes at all deeply consists in the
> doctor's examining himself, for only what he can put right
> in himself, can he hope to put right in the patient.
>
> (Jung, 1951b, p. 116)

Searles describes in exquisite detail the ways the therapist is currently 'in therapy,' going even further than Jung by suggesting that the client is also actively involved in this cure of the therapist, and needs to be to make healthy himself. Still, even in Searles' system the therapist is basically doing a continual but private 'self-analysis' in session, paying close attention to his own shifts in feeling and fantasy. In fact, Searles probably spends more time interpreting his own (counter-)transference than the client's, because 'the feelings that the therapist is having are of the very essence' of what the treatment is about (1978, p. 151). More precisely Searles declares that his ever-changing 'sense of identity' is:

... my most reliable source of data as to what is transpiring between the patient and myself, and within the patient. . . . I have described, in effect, the 'use' of such fluctuations in one's sense of identity as being a prime source of discovering, in work with a patient, not only the countertransference processes but also transferences, newly developing facets of the patient's own self-image, and so on.

(Searles, 1966–7, p. 68)

Much of this would seem to fill in Jung's more general description of countertransference as 'a highly important organ of information' (1929c, p. 71). Thus, because his own ego-boundaries are permeable, the therapist must analyze himself to understand the client. This is another way of saying that countertransference reveals transference.

About all this Jung again has a less detailed but parallel point of view. He does not hypothesize as fully as Searles how the 'self-education' of the therapist will ultimately help the client, but Jung nevertheless concludes that 'the doctor must change himself if he is to become capable of changing his patient' (1929c, p. 73). Jung tends to give this operation a moralistic or negative slant: the analyst must 'doctor himself . . . so that his personality shall not react unfavorably on the patient' (1929c, p. 73). In other words, he needs to get his illness out of the client's way. The therapist's neuroses and unconscious processes can be sensed by the client and may be the chief hindrance to progress in treatment, a point that Searles (1958a, 1961g, 1972a) repeatedly makes.

Even though Jung's is a negative injunction, as opposed to Searles' stance that the therapist should be in the way (so the client can cure him), Jung prescribes equally strong medicine for the therapist. The self-therapy of the therapist specifically

... requires the counter-application to the doctor himself of whatever system is believed in – and moreover with the same relentlessness, consistency, and perseverance with which the doctor applies it to the patient.

When one considers with what attentiveness and critical judgment the psychologist must keep track of his patients in order to show up all their false turnings, their false conclusions and infantile subterfuges, then it is truly no mean achievement for him to perform the same work upon himself.

(Jung, 1929c, p. 73)

The therapist, then, should be fair, exemplary (though not perfect), and equally involved. This note of equality highlights a subtle difference in Jung's and Searles' discussion of psychotherapy as mutual therapy. Jung insists that the therapist be as engaged as the client. As previously noted, he even says that 'a good half' of therapy is the therapist's self-examination (Jung, 1951b, p. 116). So the two participants are on an even footing. Searles' implication, however, is that most of the therapeutic examination goes on in the therapist, whose countertransference is so revealing of the client. This is not to say that the client is not equally 'participating,' but he may not be examining himself as actively or accurately as the therapist is. Another way of saying this is that most of the 'consciousness-raising' is done by the therapist. The majority of the 'insight' work is by the therapist on himself, according to Searles.

In this limited sense, therefore, Searles requires that the therapist be more 'in therapy' than Jung does. But this difference may be an artifact of Searles' particular clientele, which by and large is more disturbed than Jung's. In other words, Searles' theory may call for the therapist to be more in therapy simply because his clients cannot be – yet. They are not 'good candidates' for analysis, so to speak. Searles in fact mentions that it is only in the 'late phase' of the therapy process that the client himself is 'ready for psychoanalysis' in the sense of rigorous self-examination (1961g, p. 551). Until then, the therapist does the analysis.

This Searles–Jung difference on the degree of the therapist's in-session, self-therapy is probably unimportant and certainly unmeasurable. The important thing is that the therapist have his own reactions more or less constantly in mind. That is to say, the therapist must attend to his own 'unconscious' during therapy, not just during his own analysis or before or after the session. Searles puts this most graphically, encouraging the therapist to rely on the unconscious as 'a friend indispensable to both himself and to his patients' (1958a, p. 215). Jung adds, 'My reaction is the only thing with which I as an individual can legitimately confront the patient' (1935b, p. 5). Jung pointedly includes reactions from the unconscious of the therapist – emotions, dreams, fantasies – as key parts of the therapist's transference repertoire (1935a).

In this regard a point that both Searles and Jung implicitly emphasize is that, whether he is more 'in therapy' or not, the therapist should usually be ahead of the client in their mutual attempts to decipher or work with the unconscious. The 'ahead' here refers to sequence – the therapist is conscious first or faster – rather than to any inherent moral superiority. This situation is reminiscent of and related to Searles' concept of the client's identity being built up 'first' in the therapist, or Jung's admonition to the therapist to put aside theory and technique and 'be the man through whom you wish to influence others' (1929c, p. 73) – i.e., be it 'first'. One might say that the therapist 'precedes' the client in a number of ways, though he does not take 'precedence' over the client. And if the therapist does 'go first,' he does so in order that therapy may proceed. Furthermore, the therapist's earlier understandings or integrations have direct bearing not just on his self-therapy but on other crucial aspects of the treatment process, such as the maintenance of the therapeutic framework and the 'timing' of interpretations.

The therapist's 'earlier' arrival at certain realizations, in whatever context, points to the fact that the process of psychotherapy will always have an element of 'waiting' in it. This may mean that the therapist is waiting on the patient or vice versa. As Searles points out:

> It is not only that the patient becomes more and more able to face strong feelings but the analyst, through his experience with the patient, becomes better and better able to face them also and that he can't with his first interview.
>
> (Searles, 1980, p. 170)

'Waiting' also may mean that progress in therapy must wait. Certain things must happen first – groundwork must be laid. All this implies a time dimension, an extended treatment process that is long-term. Jung reasons that mental illnesses are 'misdevelopments that have been built up over many years. . . . Time is therefore an irreplaceable factor in healing' (1935b, p. 24). As if to corroborate this, casual research (Knight, 1965) revealed that Searles' average, usually schizophrenic, client at Chestnut Lodge had been ill for nine years and treated for the staggering number of 900 sessions.

The therapeutic environment

Since time and 'waiting' are such important dimensions of both process and cure, Jung and Searles attach primary importance to the quality of the therapeutic environment. The chief ingredient here is the overall relationship between therapist and client, the transference. The ongoing interaction of the participants makes or breaks the therapy; it is the core of the treatment process. But another crucial ingredient is that which 'holds' the transference relationship. Because the relationship must endure lengthy periods of growth, regression and waiting, Jung and Searles postulate that it requires a sort of protective container. In this regard both authors are not so much referring to literal aspects of the treatment environment (see Langs and Searles, 1980), though there are certain similarities, for example, in their predominant use of 'face-to-face' seating instead of the analytic couch (Jung, 1935a; Searles, 1965a).[3] Rather, they are referring to the creation of a safe place emotionally, in which the transference interactions can unfold. It is a kind of 'field' in which the therapeutic events can take place. In gestalt terms, it is the 'ground' for the 'figure' of the transference.

Jung and Searles have different names but similar ideas about this stabilization phenomenon which fosters the analyst–patient interchange of 'health' and 'illness.' Jung describes it under the heading of 'the rapport,'[4] adding that the client 'can win his *inner security* only from the *security of his relationship* to the doctor' (1951b, p. 116, italics mine). The therapeutic situation must be steady. Searles, following other (British) psychoanalysts, calls this solid, containing aspect of therapy the 'holding environment' (1980, p. 161). And he does not just mean that the therapist provides ongoing support for the client – he also means that the client must emotionally hold the therapist, indeed sometimes needs to do so first before he can accept the therapist's holding him (Searles, 1973a, p. 190; 1980, p. 163). This element of 'holding' by *both* participants is somewhat suggested by Jung's definition of the rapport as 'a relationship of *mutual* confidence' (1951b, p. 116, italics mine); however, Searles' emphasis on reciprocity here is much greater.

The importance of this shared, protected 'space' within which therapist and client work cannot be overestimated. Jung believes the rapport is the emotional dimension upon which the 'therapeutic success ultimately depends' (1951b). For Searles, the holding environment is an aspect of symbiosis, which in pathological form between parent and child is a cause of the illness and which in therapeutic form is a source of the cure. The therapeutic symbiosis is, furthermore, a transitional goal of treatment, according to Searles (1961g, 1975b), something that is worked toward. Once established, the individuated 'self' arises from it. Similarly, Jung (1944, p. 54) speaks of the client's repeated efforts to form a 'temenos' – a holy or safe place (literally, a courtyard or grove dedicated to the gods). This symbolic sanctuary especially needs to be established during disorienting moments in the therapy process. But Jung also feels that the secure, symbolic/emotional temenos is a particular type of 'mandala,' which, like many quadratic structures, can be a symbol of the goal of analysis as well as a compensatory reaction to the onslaught of unconscious imagos (1950b). So, creating a safe place within the therapist–client relationship is akin to cure. And developing a secure 'space' in therapy is part of several different stages in the continuing process of treatment and individuation.

From a linear perspective the therapy process looks alike for both theorists: 'holding' → symbiosis → self (Searles), 'rapport' → temenos → Self (Jung). Their difference here lies in Jung's focus on the symbolic imagery of this progression, whereas Searles' attention is more on the 'feelings' generated between client and therapist. However, many of the emotions involved in Searles' approach have symbolic reference points in the client's past: the client is re-experiencing, or experiencing for the first time now, emotions that were not fully lived then (1978). So although Searles' therapy sequence theoretically 'retraces, in reverse' the client's earlier developmental warps, it cannot really do so (1961g, p. 523). The link to the past is symbolic, because transference cannot change literal history. But transference can change emotional, unconscious history when the analyst serves as 'Good Mother,' 'Bad Mother' or 'transference father' (Searles, 1961g, 1975a); that is, when he comes to symbolize or 'be' these things. Therefore, a transference approach such as Searles', which hypothesizes correction of 'past' deprivations, is necessarily symbolic. Jung's approach only appears more symbolic, rather than interpersonal, because he does not interpret symbols as referents to a 'pre-oedipal' past, or to any past, for that matter, except the archetypal past. Jung's symbol interpretation looks forward to the 'not yet' conscious, rather than the repressed past.

From the above, it becomes evident that any separation of the 'transference' itself from what might be called the 'therapeutic framework' is an arbitrary division. The two are clearly interrelated, since both rest on emotional considerations.

'Holding,' or solid 'rapport,' shows up as the means and one of the ends of therapy. Although it would seem that a solid 'container' should precede the emotional interchange, neither is preliminary. Or else they take turns. A better frame allows for better transference, but the mutual struggle with 'sickness' and mental 'health' helps the supporting framework to grow. At bottom, framework and transference are probably twin aspects of the same thing, or perhaps the same phenomenon viewed from two perspectives.

Working with the unconscious

Up until now this discussion has centered on emotional aspects and the encounter, person-to-person, between the analyst and the patient. The dynamics of cure seem to take place most fundamentally at this 'feeling' level. The overall sense of both theorists' presentations is that analysis is first an emotional experience and only second a cognitive or 'learning' process. This is particularly true with Searles. Much as the etiology of the client's illness involves not isolated traumatic events but the subtle, longstanding influence and attitude of his family, so the therapy process is a matter of long-term, heavily nuanced, and often unconscious interaction. Therefore Searles' judgment is: 'Interpretations are important, to be sure, but of far greater importance is the emotional atmosphere or climate of the sessions, day after day, year after year' (1978, p. 44). Jung makes similar statements about therapeutic transformation via fantasy work: 'I would not give priority to understanding. . . . The important thing is not to interpret and understand . . . but to experience' (1928a, p. 213).

Nevertheless, the way both authors approach psycho-pathology – as a prevalence of highly activated, pathogenic introjects without conscious awareness – returns the argument to the question of consciousness. Furthermore, their definitions of health emphasize change or growth in consciousness as much as anything else. It seems, then, that the key to the fuller 'experience' they advocate lies in fuller, non-repressive awareness. Experience is already there as potential, waiting to be discovered.

The act of separating experience from awareness, or 'atmosphere' from 'interpretation,' is, like many differentiations, a somewhat arbitrary process. The primacy that Jung and Searles seem to attribute to 'feeling' processes and the therapist–client relationship may be a function of the ease with which such affectively based matters can be abandoned by therapist and client alike. The client, after all, comes to therapy with a rather shrunken life experience, often due to habitually defensive attitudes toward his own experience. This characteristic 'psychic inertia' of which both Jung and Searles speak (see Chapter 3, p. 67) is reinforced by two factors the client shares with mankind in general: anxiety concerning change of any sort (Searles, 1961d) and resistance to conscious experience (Jung, 1935a). Meanwhile, for the analyst, consciousness-raising can easily devolve into protective, mechanical abstraction, particularly when the emotional interchanges with the client become increasingly taxing personally. Thus Searles' and Jung's real objections are not toward awareness, by any means, but toward intellectualization in client and therapist, and toward defensive pretensions to 'neutrality' or omniscient authority in the therapist alone. In psychotherapy, 'experience' and 'awareness' are not antitheses, but 'experience' and 'intellectualization' are.

From a more comprehensive perspective, where awareness and experience are allies rather than opposites, analysis can be seen as a two-tiered process of relationship *and* interpretation. Interpretation must indeed follow or arise from relationship, but, to meet the authors' criteria for 'health,' understanding is also of the essence. What ultimately makes the therapist–client interaction different from the past and applicable to the future is that intimate experience can now be scrutinized on a regular (and contained) basis. The 'new' thing in therapy is the therapist's willingness to engage the client emotionally (which in itself may be corrective) plus his effort to understand what is happening between them (an awareness attempt in which the client soon joins, one hopes, via the working alliance). These two therapeutic measures act directly on and correspond structurally to psychopathology (dissociated introjects without consciousness) and to the process goal of 'symbol-repair' (multiple selves with consciousness). In the infectious transference the disorganized inner selves catch (or are caught by) the analyst, who accepts and tries to understand. The therapy, pathology and goals therefore fit together, forming the dynamic of cure.

If relationship and rapport underlie the entire therapy process, it is evident that the greater awareness evolving through transference predominates during the later stages. This is the phase where symbol-repair becomes complete. At this point interpretative understanding of the introjects and complexes becomes not only paramount but, indeed, sometimes possible for the first time. While this process is not always sequential, since analysis actually will consist of small, successive relationship ↔ interpretation increments, the general trend is: relationship first, then interpretation. Relationship means intimate involvement between analyst and patient, or more specifically between their introjects. Without this 'reality' basis, interpretations are bodiless, written on water. Interpretation, however, is the crucial 'follow through' on the emotional interchange in transference. While not quite so heavily accented by Searles and Jung, it is still a necessity.

Cognitive work and interpretation provide many things. First, and sometimes most important, interpretation demonstrates empathy (or the attempt at empathy, which can be the main thing). With accurate interpretation also comes a sense of termination: the particular issue, complex or emotion of the moment now feels 'closed,' even if only temporarily. Effective interpretation also marks the transition to the next psychological moment or issue. With one aspect dealt with, a new or deeper one may emerge. Interpretative understanding is also transitional on a wider scale: an overall understanding of what has happened and what can and does happen to the client is what he takes with him at the end of therapy. He has the pre-therapy experience and the therapist–client experience, and he may leave therapy once he has truly understood both these things. In a sense, interpretation looks backwards and forwards: showing what has happened but pointing to the next development.

Focusing on the interpretation of events shifts the discussion of 'the process of psychotherapy' to a more cognitive basis. Therapist–client transactions burrow to the heart of the therapeutic experience, while interpretation touches the mind. Likewise, discussion of transference centers attention on underlying processes in psychotherapy, while discussion of interpretation focuses on more directly observable processes. And in analysis itself the act of interpretation consists of making underlying processes more observable and better understood.

Another way of looking at interpretation, then, is to find out how Searles and Jung actually work with 'unconscious' contents (the unknown, unseen). Unconscious communications, unconscious selves, the analyst's own 'unconscious' – all these and more have been featured in the transference discussion. Clearly a major way the unconscious is realized is in the mixing of the personalities. Here the therapist gets the client's unconscious directly, so to speak. But Jung and Searles also explore less direct expressions of the client's personality that are not necessarily transferred to the therapist for 'in vivo' experiencing. These indirect expressions are the symbolic, unconscious products that the client reveals in dreams, symptoms and words.

Working with the patient's unconscious material essentially means working with his fantasies. Searles and Jung both hold spontaneous, symbolic activity in very high esteem. Searles states:

> Much of the fascination involved in conducting a psycho-analysis, as well as much of the attendant anxiety, has to do with the glimpses one gains of the patient's unconscious fantasies, glimpses provided by his gestures and the changes in his posture, by the special intonations of his words, by odd word usages or slips of the tongue, by brief but highly significant pauses.
>
> (Searles, 1973b, p. 267)

Jung states his position as follows:

> I have no small opinion of fantasy. To me, it is the maternally creative side of the masculine mind. When all is said and done, we can never rise above fantasy. . . . All the works of man have their origin in creative imagination.
>
> (Jung, 1931f, p. 45)

If the above statements by Searles and Jung indicate a favorable, or at least highly interested, approach to fantasy, they also highlight certain differences in emphasis. Searles' statement already lets one know that the realm of unconscious fantasy is expressed most fruitfully by verbal and non-verbal gestures in the waking world, and particularly in therapy sessions. He speaks of unconscious fantasy, but then moves away quickly from a focus on 'fantasies' as such. Instead he looks for indicators ('glimpses') that unconscious fantasy is going on. Jung's focus, on the other hand, is more on 'pure' fantasies, on symbolic or imaginal products ('creative imagination'). Another contrast, though it is not explicitly stated in the quotation above, is that Jung (1916a,

1934c, 1944) places paramount importance on non-waking and/or extra-therapy fantasy, especially dreams.

The passages quoted above also suggest a fundamentally different evaluation of fantasy overall. Searles' statement immediately cites the burden ('anxiety') of working with unconscious fantasy, while Jung's practically declares fantasy the source of civilization ('all the works of man'). Jung's statement, 'I have no small opinion of fantasy,' is a classic understatement, as he goes on to show.

Jung's extremely high evaluation of fantasy does not imply that Searles' is a devaluation. These are merely differences of degree. There may in fact be very practical reasons why Searles centers his attention on the less 'fantastic,' in-session gestures of clients. First, Searles finds that pure fantasy is often repressed by clients of all types, chiefly in order to retain a pathologically symbiotic relation with the therapist (1973b, p. 268). Therefore, since there is no spontaneous expression of the imagination in its natural form, it must be inferred via 'glimpses' or even transferred to the therapist. Second, Searles' emphasis may be different from Jung's for theoretical reasons. Recalling Chapter 2, Searles makes the paradoxical suggestion that severely psychotic patients have no fantasy life (1962a). They are dedifferentiated to such a degree that fantasy/reality distinctions are nonexistent. On the one hand, there is no fantasy as such and, on the other, behaviors and perceptions of such clients become symbolically charged. These clients are too disturbed to fantasize and, since there is no fantasy to interpret, only their gestures and odd communications remain.

Therefore, Searles' approach to obtaining unconscious material is probably quite pragmatic. Yet this is interestingly complemented by Jung's belief that purely symbolic fantasy is also inherently practical. Aside from the previously mentioned benefits to mankind in general, Jung cites the imagination's contribution to the therapy process:

> The scientific credo of our time has developed a superstitious phobia about fantasy. But the real is what works. And the fantasies of the unconscious work, there can be no doubt about that. . . . Something works behind the veil of fantastic images, whether we give this something a good or bad name.
>
> (Jung, 1928a, p. 217)

For Jung, fantasy is effective and helpful, in and of itself. For Searles, being able to fantasize at all may be an indication of therapeutic progress in cases of severe pathology.

So far, it looks like Searles finds fantasy in treatment 'reality,' so to speak, whereas Jung finds it in the client's actually reported 'fantasies.' However, there is for Searles another locus of unconscious material – hallucinations – which bridges some of that 'reality vs. pure fantasy' gap and makes his position more compatible with Jung's. What the dream is to Jung (1934c, p. 142) – the chief expression of the unconscious 'as it is' – the hallucination is to Searles. And if Jung is primarily a dream-interpreter, Searles is an hallucination-interpreter.

The differences between dream and hallucination are ultimately not very wide. Searles repeatedly provides and interprets examples of hallucinated experiences that seem quite congruent with dream material: terrifying figures peering in the window, exploding teeth in the room, a young girl in the closet pleading for rescue. In addition, visual distortions of people and things in 'here and now' reality (e.g., the therapist, the building) are indicative of inner states (Searles, 1960, 1962a, 1972a). Searles summarizes this as follows:

> All of outer reality becomes kaleidoscopically changed because of the impact upon it of the patient's unconscious feelings. That is, what are essentially inner emotional changes are experienced as perceptual changes in the surrounding world.
>
> (Searles, 1967a, p. 13)

Carrying the dream/hallucination parallel still further, Searles suggests that the psychogenesis of 'delusions' is analogous to that of dreams (1952, p. 49).

From Searles' perspective, then, hallucinations come close to dreams and progress occurs when a client can dream rather than hallucinate (Searles, 1976b, p. 596). Jung's approach to fantasy involves the same thing only in the opposite direction: one of his goals in working with dreams is to make them more real, more 'present.' One way to do this is by painting, modeling in clay, dancing or somehow concretizing the images (Jung, 1931f, 1935a). Furthermore, in another version of this so-called 'active imagination' process, Jung encourages the client to amplify a fragment of a dream or spontaneous fantasy by focusing attention on it (1916a,

1928a). The process sounds somewhat like role-playing or daydreaming, except in Jung's version the image must be permitted to move autonomously, and the person must respond authentically and actively (hence, 'active' imagination).

Lest active imagination sounds like a fairly routine procedure, Jung specifies that it should be done in the company of a therapist, since it may in some cases unleash a condition that 'cannot be easily distinguished from schizophrenia' (1916a, p. 68). In a later work, Jung terms active imagination an 'anticipated psychosis' and notes that the individual (hopefully) 'is integrating the same fantasy-material to which the insane person falls victim' (1955–6, p. 531). Active imagination, then, is 'for keeps,' a kind of applied schizophrenia that can produce the real thing. In short, Jung wants his clients virtually to hallucinate in a controlled way, or at least come close to that sort of psychic reality. As with Searles, dream and hallucination are drawn together. Just as an hallucination is truly a 'waking dream,' fantasy is a waking reality.

Searles derives unconscious material from hallucinations and Jung from dreams and quasi-hallucinations – but how do they interpret such products? A preliminary question arises, though, as to the necessity of interpretation at all. As previously discussed, Searles believes that interpretation holds a lesser place than the 'atmosphere' prevalent in the therapist–client relationship (1978, p. 44). He further suggests that interpretations have approximately the same importance in therapy as childhood traumata (i.e., once considered central, now less so). Therefore interpretation, like trauma theory, appears to be somewhat obsolete technically in Searles' view. Jung too gives interpretation short shrift, at least when therapy calls for a 'real settlement' by the client with his unconscious:

> It is not a question of interpretation: it is a question of releasing unconscious processes and letting them come into the conscious mind in the form of fantasies. We can try our hand at interpreting these fantasies if we like. . . . But it is of vital importance that he [the client] should experience them to the full.
>
> (Jung, 1928a, p. 217)

Later Jung adds that it is the 'continual conscious realization of unconscious fantasies, together with active participation in the fantastic events' that results in growth and change (p. 219). His emphasis here is on awareness and engagement, rather than interpretation in the usual sense of translating symbols into other terms.

Though interpretation is decidedly secondary, it turns out to be necessary after all – for the analyst. It would be too much to say that interpretation is solely for the analyst's benefit, not the patient's. Jung and Searles are not proposing that interpretation is some sort of theoretical game or mental exercise for the analyst. However, it is clear that the analyst often understands the client in a different, sometimes deeper way than the client understands himself. Otherwise there would be no question about the 'timing' of interpretations – 'when' to offer them to the patient. Furthermore, if client and analyst viewed the client in exactly the same way, there also would probably be no issues around 'resistance' (see below).

Yet interpretative understanding may be for the analyst's, and ultimately the client's, benefit in the sense that the analyst needs constantly to interpret in order to participate effectively in the cure via transference. That is, if the analyst is, as Searles hypothesizes, molding a unified self-image of the client that the latter can re-introject, the analyst must be able to interpret the diverse emotional fragments and introjects being transferred into him. He has to get the picture. Failing that, neither analyst nor client will have any idea what is going on. As Jung's earlier quoted statement suggests, 'The doctor's knowledge . . . is the one dim light in the darkness' (1946, p. 199). Interpretations are really signposts to the analyst, subject periodically to the client's assent, that the analyst is comprehending the client accurately. So, while the goal of therapy for the client – less pathological 'selves' with conscious awareness – demands his increased self-understanding, the integration of the client by the analyst demands interpretations. What the analyst gives back to the client may be something different from what the analyst has integrated: the client receives the end product rather than the intermediate steps. Hence, the implicit conclusion from all this is that therapy will fail without the analyst's ongoing interpretations, voiced or not.

Thus interpretations do after all turn out to be necessary, and evidently the therapist may make them as wildly, tentatively, bluntly or deeply as he wants to – to himself. How he presents them to the client is another matter. The timing, presentation and assimilation of interpretations are areas in which Jung and Searles are in some agreement.

Despite the secondary status that Jung and Searles in some ways give to interpretation of the unconscious, they both interpret often. 'Often' here is relative, of course, to an analytic stance in which the analyst typically is silent, 'neutral' and gives interpretative statements rarely, usually at the end of a session. Tied in with their greater frequency of interpretations is a humble assumption, even expectation, that some of them will be wrong. Searles says with some sense of relief:

> I make far more interpretations with various of my patients than most people would – far more, so that my patients are relatively content that some of my comments are useful and others aren't. . . . And how long a time it took for me, many years, to become loosened up enough to make an interpretation within the first few seconds of the beginning of a session, for example.
>
> (Searles, 1980, p. 99)

Jung in general appears to be similarly 'loose' with his patients: 'I expose myself completely and react with no restriction' (1935a, p. 139). While this may be a slight overstatement, it must be assumed to apply to interpretations of their unconscious material as well. Jung confirms this assumption in discussing dream interpretation:

> Not only do I give the patient an opportunity to find associations to his dreams, I give myself the same opportunity. Further, I present him with my ideas and opinions. . . . No harm is done if now and then one goes astray in this riddle-reading: sooner or later the psyche will reject the mistake, much as the organism rejects a foreign body.
>
> (Jung, 1931f, pp. 44–5)

Moreover, Jung adds that proving his interpretations 'right' would be 'a pretty hopeless undertaking anyway' (1931f). Thus, Jung and Searles both believe that interpretative mistakes are inevitable and without long-term harm.

If the two theorists seem to be reasonably relaxed about interpretation, this does not imply that they are careless about it. Both Jung and Searles stress a specific tailoring of interpretations to fit the capacities, needs and style of the client. For instance, Jung takes into account the client's 'type' – introvert or extrovert – and adjusts his interpretations accordingly to the 'subjective' (inner facts) or 'objective' (outer facts) level (1928a). He also considers such client vectors as age, degree of pathology, state of consciousness and so on (1961a) – in fact Jung's whole interpretative standpoint is so individualized that the therapist 'should in every single case be ready to construct a totally new theory' (Jung, 1934c, p. 147). Similarly, Searles suggests that interpretations, to be effective, must be made in the client's own vocabulary and affective style – angry, tentative, hopeless, or whatever (1978). Also he feels that interpretations should correspond stylistically to the developmental phase then being analyzed: 'oral'-feeding, 'anal'-cathartic, etc. While Searles and Jung obviously have different theoretical vantage points (e.g., 'introvert' vs. 'anal'), it is nevertheless true that both are quite sensitive to the client's state of mind.

This interpretative delicacy extends to the issue of 'resistance,' or non-acceptance of a particular interpretation. A not uncommon point of view is that the client's refusal to believe or understand an interpretation is defensively oriented: the client cannot tolerate the interpretation. Within this tautology, resistance 'proves' that the interpretation is in fact correct (otherwise, it wouldn't be resisted). Jung and Searles, however, reject this circular argument. In their view, if a client is resistant, he may be defensive but appropriately so. Jung points out two possible 'interpretations' of resistance itself: 1) the client is not yet able to understand the therapist's comment or 2) the interpretation is wrong (1961a, p. 220). Searles likewise states that the patient will come to the interpretation (if it is correct) at his own speed, and adds that the therapist's attempt to rush things is probably a reflection of his own resistance (1978, pp. 50–1). That is, unable to tolerate the impact and reality-nuclei of the client's projections, the therapist quickly interprets them back to the client.

Overall, it appears that for Searles and Jung, voiced interpretations should always be in service of, rather than against, the client. As Searles cogently explains, the analyst needs to work with the client to understand the client's reality, instead of 'pounding against' resistance and 'brainwashing' the client into a pathological compliance with the therapist's reality (1978, pp. 45, 50). Jung's conclusions on dream analysis strike a similar chord on the client's behalf:

In the end it makes very little difference whether the doctor understands or not, but it makes all the difference whether the patient understands ... every dream interpretation [is] invalid until such time as a formula is found which wins the assent of the patient.

(Jung, 1934c, pp. 146–7)

In this sense, a resisted interpretation is a wrong interpretation.

The proper criterion for the correctness of an interpretation is the client's acceptance of it. But the way acceptances or rejections are actually communicated back to the therapist are points on which Jung and Searles coincide and differ. Jung looks directly to the patient's unconscious for confirmation, especially to the succeeding dreams:

If we make a wrong interpretation, or if it is somehow incomplete, we may be able to see it from the next dream. Thus, for example, the earlier motif may be repeated in clearer form, or our interpretation may be deflated by some ironic paraphrase, or it may meet with straightforward violent opposition.

(Jung, 1917, p. 111)

If the reinterpretation then fails, however, Jung thinks it will be indicated more in the conscious feelings that both patient and therapist have of 'boredom ... doubt ... deadlock ... and mutual desiccation' – that is, a therapeutic impasse (p. 112). Searles also turns to the client for verification, but he turns first to his conscious reactions:

There are a number of safeguards. One, a patient who is able to tell me when something is quite off the mark ... consciously able to tell me that that is irrelevant to the best of his knowledge at the moment.... I find that reassuring that such a patient is not going to be likely to become compliantly conforming to some unconscious fantasies of mine.

(Searles, 1980, p. 98)

In contrast to Jung, Searles does not appear to refer to subsequent fantasies that may follow the therapist's interpretation of a fantasy. This is surprising in light of the fact that Searles (1961b, 1961d) frequently interprets references to people, places and eras outside of therapy as disguised commentaries on the actual therapist–client interactions of the moment (i.e., in talking about the landlord, for instance, the client may really be referring to the therapist).[5]

Jung's and Searles' procedures for presenting and gaining acceptance of interpretations correspond closely, but their positions on the content of interpretations diverge. Basically, their differing views of the unconscious color their interpretations accordingly. A major distinction arises from Jung's hypothesis of a collective unconscious, for which there is no close parallel in Searles' concept of the unconscious. Searles tends to make 'transference interpretations' – these refer mostly to repetitions and reparations of past emotional contexts which are embodied now in the analyst–patient relationship (1959c, p. 310). Besides this, the 'weirdness' of schizophrenic communications is sometimes such that the analyst must, in effect, interpret moment-by-moment statements and behaviors simply to make them understandable at all (Searles, 1961e, p. 475). Searles calls these 'action interpretations' (1961g, p. 528). In contrast, Jung's analyses veer toward the archetypal perspective, incorporating the compensatory, guiding and prospective trends of an ages-old, creative unconscious (1948a). Jung looks to the unconscious for hints toward the future, whereas Searles looks for explanatory principles within the more recent history of family and infancy.

Another way of defining their fundamental interpretative differences is highlighted by Jung's statement on introjects: 'I am looking for what the *unconscious is doing* with the complexes' (1935a, p. 84). Searles, on the other hand, is looking *for* the introjects revealed by unconscious fantasy. His unconscious is a more static 'place,' where emotions can be identified and elucidated; Jung's unconscious is not only a quasi-physical space but a dynamic – an 'energic' phenomenon or source (Jung, 1928b, p. 4).

Some examples will make these distinctions clearer. Searles interprets a schizophrenic woman's dream that 'They had taken out all my teeth and put people in place of them and then ground them down' as follows:

> She began to realize, in a figurative sense, what was being literally expressed in the dream; the fact of herself having 'ground down' – so to speak – persons close to her, with an

extremely powerful and persistent castrativeness. Significantly, I had been feeling unusually ground down by her during one hour on the preceding day – the day of the dream. But she was still far from being able to accept her own wish to do this to me and to others. Instead, the potential realization presented itself to her in thrice-disguised form.

(Searles, 1962a, pp. 567–8n)

This 'hostility' interpretation emphasizes the past, the counter-transference, the 'wish' and the disguise.

In contrast is Jung's interpretation of a young client's dream about his highly successful father, whom the client openly admired. In a dream the client raged at his father, who had crashed the car and was 'dead drunk':

If his relation to the father is in fact good, why must the dream manufacture such an improbable story in order to discredit the father? ... The answer in this case would be that his unconscious is obviously trying to take the father down a peg. If we regard this as a compensation, we are forced to the conclusion that his relation to his father is not only good, but actually too good. ... His father is still too much the guarantor of his existence, and the dreamer is still living what I would call the provisional life ... the compensation is entirely to the point, since it forces the son to contrast himself with his father, which is the only way he could become conscious of himself.

(Jung, 1934c, pp. 154–5)

Jung's interpretation is based not on hostility toward the father but on: 1) an apparently helpful suggestion from the unconscious, 2) the dreamer's current psychological condition and 3) the direction he should take in the future regarding his individuation and his 'father complex.'

From the above examples it is evident that Searles emphasizes defensive functions when explaining the formation and structure of unconscious fantasy. In fact it is the degree of defensiveness that results in the corresponding bizarreness of the fantasy experience (Searles, 1961c). That is, an intolerable feeling or thought is first repressed, but then shows up disguised and distorted in and by the fantasy. In contrast Jung sees symbolic fantasy as a colorful, primitive language that appeals directly to emotion (1961a). Therefore according to Jung, 'A symbol does not disguise, it reveals in time' (p. 212).

Searles, however, does not always interpret fantasy as a defensive operation. His interpretations frequently seem to lie closer to Jung's definition of the dream as 'a spontaneous self-portrayal, in symbolic form, of the actual situation in the unconscious' (1948a, p. 263). Particularly relevant to this more existential approach to fantasy is Searles' theoretical position on the 'reality nuclei' in client projections (1976a, p. 532). For instance, if there are, as he suggests, 'evident connections between ... delusions and realistic components' of the therapist's personality (1972a, p. 203), then it follows that delusional fantasies are not necessarily so delusional (in the sense of 'distorted'). While fantasies disguise, they may also reflect the client's unconscious beliefs in the only visible way, given his dedifferentiated state, he knows how. Searles' increasing attention over the years to 'the awesome extent to which the reality of the analyst's personality gives rise to the whole, seemingly so delusional, world of the patient' (1972a, p. 211; see also 1975a, 1976c, 1978) thus seems to shift toward Jung's more phenomenological approach to fantasy as revealing 'the inner truth and reality of the patient as it is' (1934c, p. 142). In other words, Searles joins Jung in emphasizing the symbolic truth rather than the distortions in fantasy.

Further parallels crop up in some examples Searles and Jung give of dream interpretation (usually at their own expense). These examples suggest the homeostatic functions of fantasies. Discussing his own feelings of 'omnipotence,' Searles relates the following dream:

> One thing that helped me to reach some healthy perspective on the latter [his omnipotence] was a dream in which a witty and perceptive close friend and colleague, standing across the room and looking at me thoughtfully, raised the question, 'Harold, I wonder whether what you have is *omnipotence*, or *ominous impotence*?'
>
> (Searles, 1965b, p. 35)

This is a good example of what Jung would call the 'compensating function of the unconscious' (1948a, p. 244). Searles also describes another similar sort of corrective dream, this time with reference to his treatment of a psychotic client he considered violent:

I dreamed that he and I were fighting, and I was reacting to him as being – as I in waking life was then considering him to be – a dangerous, uncontrollable person. In the course of this dream-struggle he got his hands on a knifelike letter-opener. But what then happened, as I was astounded to recall upon awakening, was that *he* took *me* into custody; he, functioning as a kind of sheriff's deputy, was marching me out to turn me over to the authorities.

(Searles, 1958a, p. 203)

Searles credits this 'instructive dream' with helping him realize that it was his own murderous rage toward the patient that he feared (1958a). Thus the dream appropriately compensates a countertransference attitude, and points toward an improved future attitude.

It is not only Searles who has treatment-related dreams. Jung mentions a therapeutic impasse that was solved by his dream of a woman sitting in the 'top-most tower' of a castle:

In order to see her properly I had to bend my head back so far that I got a crick in my neck. Even in my dream I recognized the woman as my patient. From this I concluded that if I had to look up so much in the dream, I must obviously have looked down on my patient in reality.

(Jung, 1917, p. 112)

Jung then proceeded to tell the client the dream and his interpretation, with the reported result that 'treatment shot ahead beyond all expectations' (1917).

There are still other interpretative dimensions, especially in terms of dreams, along which Jung and Searles agree. Related to compensation is Jung's belief that unconscious fantasy should be interpreted in light of its purpose rather than its antecedents. Jung terms this standpoint one of 'finality,' as opposed to 'causality,' and notes, 'All psychological phenomena have some such sense of purpose inherent in them' (1948a, p. 241). This includes, of course, fantasy products, with which Jung is sometimes more concerned, in his words, with 'what for?' than 'why?' (1934c, p. 143). Although Searles tends to consider the 'why?' more than Jung does, Searles also interprets fantasy in terms of its momentary goals for the client. The unconscious goal of restitution, for instance, is evidenced in Searles' analysis of paranoid fantasy. A client's idea, for instance, of an 'all-embracing plot by the communists, the Mafia, or whatnot . . . as centering on himself' has the effect of organizing his chaotic world, however delusionally, into a coherent frame of reference (1967a, p. 15). It is also an unconscious effort to counteract feelings of insignificance (i.e., a compensation). This symbolic attempt at reordering and rebuilding is roughly parallel to Jung's previously noted belief that balanced, mandala symbols appear in clients' fantasies during moments of anxiety and disintegration (1950b). The purpose in both paranoid and mandala imagery is to maintain some integrity of the personality.

These shared ideas about purposiveness also extend to sexual fantasy. Classic psychoanalytic interpretation of fantasy frequently involves the reduction of manifestly nonsexual fantasy to 'latent,' sexual components. While Jung and Searles both regard human sexuality as a crucial, though not *the* crucial, dimension of human life, they sometimes interpret sexual imagery as having a nonsexual purpose. Jung suggests that, more often than not, sexual fantasy is simply the symbolic form that creative fantasy takes (1913, 1946). Therefore such fantasies may be symbolic of, for example, integrations or unions with self or others (or the need for same). By the same token, Searles suggests that such behaviors on the part of a schizophrenic patient can be viewed as a purposeful 'last-ditch attempt to make or maintain contact with outer reality, or with his own inner self' (1961c, p. 441).

Furthermore, both authors again apply this goal-oriented format to the therapist as well, using the same language almost word for word. Erotic fantasies toward a withdrawn client may represent 'an unconscious effort to bridge the psychological gulf between them, when more highly refined means have failed' (Searles, 1961c, p. 441). According to Jung, when therapist–client 'rapport' is poor, the therapist may have sexual fantasies 'in order to cover the distance and to build a bridge' between them (1935a, p. 144). Thus sexual fantasy is desexualized by Searles and Jung, serving client, analyst and treatment in the same compensatory fashion that all fantasies can.

Jung and Searles also agree that, when interpreting any kind of fantasy, the people and places that occur should be viewed primarily as subjective aspects of the person having the fantasy. This concept is linked to their larger hypothesis (see Chapter 2) that personality is pluralistic, composed of semi- but not totally unified 'selves.' These selves, as Jung (1934a) notes, are the characters in dreams. Searles puts the matter exclusively:

> Every dream figure – no matter how physically unlike the patient – can be found to represent the patient's portrayal of some aspect of his personality; that is, the dream figure can be found to represent a 'self-image.'
>
> (Searles, 1949/79, p. 175)

Jung's description of 'interpretation on the subjective level' agrees with Searles':

> The whole dream work is essentially subjective, and a dream is a theater in which the dreamer is himself the scene, the player, the prompter, the producer.... Such an interpretation, as the term implies, conceives of all the figures in the dream as personified features of the dreamer's own personality.
>
> (Jung, 1948a, p. 266)

However, this picture of 'subjectivity' is clouded by a number of contradictions. First, the subject/object contamination (see Chapter 2) in projections complicates matters. Imagos are not 'purely' subjective. Second, even some of the dream examples cited earlier seem to incorporate external factors like the relationship or treatment as a whole. In fact just as Searles seems to devote increasing attention to the essential accuracy of the client's most delusional fantasies, so Jung also encourages 'objective' interpretations at times. Such interpretations 'equate the dream images with real objects' (1917, p. 84).

In the final analysis, though, both theorists bring their emphases back to the subjective level of interpretation anyway. Jung, after venturing the rule that objective interpretations are called for if the fantasy-figure is an important person in the patient's life, adds, 'Even where the objective interpretation is advisable, it is well to consider also a subjective possibility' (1928–30, p. 26). Here and elsewhere, Jung appears to favor the subjective method, the introverted approach. Searles seems to conclude that the 'subject vs. object' conflict in the transference is rectified by the therapist's return of the projective burden to the client: why does the client choose to relate to or project onto this particular reality-component of the therapist (1949/79, p. 182)? Also relevant is Searles' concept that the client must eventually re-introject the healthy self-image that was consolidated first in the therapist (1958a).

Based on the fact that Searles and Jung make 'objective' interpretations, especially about the treatment itself, the overall conclusion is as follows. Theoretically, they prescribe the subjective mode, but in practice they often use the objective method as well. Appropriately enough, their most frequent references to objective interpretations are also references to therapy situations.

Depending on the perspective of the moment, for both theorists fantasy can reveal the unconscious as it is, or the unconscious's view of the objective world. In terms of treatment, unconscious fantasy may also serve as a 'measure' of progress. The relationship of mandala symbols to Jung's view of the goals of treatment and the individuation process has already been discussed: they point to a preexistent but to-be-discovered wholeness of personality. But Jung also indicates that fantasy material may mark a turning point at any stage of treatment. As usual, Jung's favorite fantasy mode is the dream. Certain dreams may show that therapy has progressed to a deep transference involvement between client and therapist (Jung, 1946, p. 183). Some dreams herald the acceptance of personal 'shadow' complexes (Jung, 1944, p. 177), while others point to regressive rather than progressive movements in general (Jung, 1944, p. 115). Hermaphroditic symbols of a refined type may indicate the end of treatment (Jung, 1946, p. 316). Jung also suggests that a client's initial dreams are valid measures of whether client and therapist are well matched and whether treatment will progress at all (1934c, p. 144). The particulars of all these symbolic signposts are too varied to delineate here. Suffice it to say that Jung pays minute attention to fantasy indicators and trusts the unconscious to portray the situation accurately.

As would be expected, Searles' use of fantasy as a measure is less detailed, more oriented toward hallucinations and the therapist's fantasies, and a little less concerned with fantasy contents as such. Given his belief that severely psychotic clients cannot 'fantasize' at all, it makes sense that Searles considers the achievement of the ability to fantasize (from the previously 'desymbolized' state) to be a progress indicator (1962a, pp. 578–80). In a similarly general way, Searles cites the increasingly synthesized hallucinations of a client as an indication of improved 'ego integration' (1972a, p. 218). More precisely,

Searles notes that the therapist's fantasies of happily nursing the infant/client are signs of arrival at the promising stage of 'therapeutic symbiosis' (1961g, p. 540). The capacity of both therapy participants to playfully fantasize and 'mix-up' reality and fantasy is also a sign of that necessary stage of therapeutic growth (1961g).

Searles' most distinctive use of fantasy as measure is, like Jung's, in the realm of dreams. He particularly mentions the 'recovery dream,' in which crucial growth in the patient's 'self-esteem' is symbolically expressed (Searles, 1960, p. 262). For example, dream images can show: the triumph of the patient's 'healthy self' over the 'neurotic self,' a human self-conception emerging over a patient's nonhuman one, a freedom from symptoms, or an establishment of a person's true gender identity (Searles, 1960, pp. 262–4). In all these cases, Searles is interpreting dreams not in retrospect or in terms of anticipated goals but as measures of current progress.

Even in the actual process, in session, of working with fantasy, there is at least one instance where Searles and Jung agree. When interpreting dreams, Jung espouses a controlled associational technique he calls 'establishing the context' (1934c, p. 149). Instead of freely associating from the image, the patient stays in contact with the original image. Otherwise, in Jung's view, the client will stray from the dream itself and its message. Searles customarily uses free associational technique in working with clients (1951), but he mentions one occasion where he found 'directed' associations of use to himself (1952, p. 86). By returning his free associations, whenever they got too 'free,' to the issue at hand, Searles was able to elucidate the countertransference. Along these same lines, Searles' continual use of countertransference responses, including his own fantasies, to all his clients' material is fairly congruent with Jung's (1931f, 1935a) techniques of reacting without restriction and providing his own associations to the client's fantasy products. Both theorists, then, actively use their own reactions to formulate and interpret their clients' fantasies.

For all their similarities in working with the unconscious, at bottom Jung and Searles have different, though perhaps complementary, approaches overall. In a number of ways it is evident that Searles' basic thrust is to bring 'fantasy' back to 'reality.' This may take the form of relating fantasies to the client's actual 'past' or to his repressed emotions, or interpreting fantasy in light of the treatment situation itself. Thus, fantasy work leans toward 'here and now' practicalities – 'real' life. Searles does not denigrate fantasy by any means, but he wants to find out what it reveals. He 'uses' it. Jung does these things too, only there is also an element in Jung of leaving fantasy alone. That is, although he wants fantasy to relate to reality and be treated as a 'reality,' Jung sometimes wants it to have its own reality. Therefore, some of Jung's program involves taking fantasy farther 'out' – amplifying it or going farther into the unconscious with it. Particularly as related to archetypal fantasies, Jung suggests 'dreaming the myth onwards,' expanding the unconscious fantasy but not necessarily translating it into other terms (1940, p. 160).

This non-interpretive viewpoint is clearly related to Jung's stance on 'active imagination' (1916a, 1928a). In both instances the hypothesis of a mythological, collective unconscious is the foundation for the non-translation of fantasies and for Jung's differences with Searles. Since the archetypal unconscious is not personal, there is simply no personal history to translate such fantasies back into. In contrast, Searles' 'unconscious' is derived from personal history, so the client's fantasies can be reduced to their personal antecedents. Both theorists are consistent in their applications; they merely have different assumptions about the unconscious.

Yet even here they are not entirely at odds. Theoretically, Searles' belief that the unconscious has strictly personal reference points implies that the unconscious is finite and could therefore be fully analyzed. However, Searles also notes that it is impossible for anyone to be 'free of an unconscious' (1978, p. 110). This echoes Jung's opinion that 'The unconscious as we know can never be "done with" once and for all' (1951a, p. 20).

Another reason perhaps why Searles' orientation is toward reality and Jung's is toward the reality of fantasy is, once again, Searles' largely schizophrenic clientele. Jung (1946) stresses the importance of having a firmly established ego before embarking on these fantasy excursions; Searles is concerned with his clients having any workable ego-identity at all. The latter's clients often do not know if they are fantasizing or not. Likewise, while Jung's 'individuation' involves the relativization or detachment of the ego, Searles' involves the formation of one. From another standpoint one could say that Searles' clients are too deeply submerged in what Jung would call the collective unconscious. They cannot get out, whereas Jung's clients are sometimes trying to get in (temporarily at least).

Stages of therapy

The endpoints of the process of psychotherapy have been discussed, as have the means, both underlying and more visible, to those ends. What remains is to delineate the usual order of events in the process, a kind of overview or blueprint of psycho-therapy. This raises some difficulties, however. Just as this chapter does not present a sequential description of the process from beginning to end of therapy, neither do Jung and Searles make such a description.

The difficulty is that there is no consistently occurring series of happenings. The process of analysis, for Jung and Searles, does not seem to 'progress' in a logical, neat fashion. As described earlier, therapy sequences move forwards and backwards, or backwards in order to go forwards, or sometimes in a seemingly circular motion. Linear paradigms are difficult to construct without doing damage to the phenomenological realities. As Jung laments:

> In our observation of individual cases there is a bewildering number of variations as well as the greatest arbitrariness in the sequence of states, despite all agreement in principle as to the basic facts. A logical order, as we understand it, or even the possibility of such an order, seems to lie outside the bounds of our subject at present.
>
> (Jung, 1946, pp. 321–2)

Nevertheless, both authors try. Jung offers two quasi-textbook models of the therapy sequence at a general level for which there is no parallel in Searles. Jung first presents a paradigm based on patients. That is, he describes the 'many layers' of the therapy process and how they correspond 'to the diversities of the patients requiring treatment' (1935b, pp. 19–20). Some patients merely need some 'good advice.' A second group needs to make a 'thorough confession.' At a deeper level are those who need a 'reductive analysis' of the Freudian or Adlerian type. Finally, when the third stage results in 'repetitions' or 'standstill,' a 'dialectical procedure' is demanded and the fourth stage, 'individuation,' commences.

The above model at times confuses types of clients with phases of therapy. A more consistent paradigm is one Jung develops based strictly on methods (1929c). Jung describes a sequence of stages one client might go through in therapy. The first stage is *confession and catharsis*. The second stage is *elucidation*, which explains in Freudian terms 'why' the client was ill. Once things have been explained, however, it is necessary to find practical ways to adapt normally – the *education* stage. For those who need more than normality there is a fourth stage, *transformation*, which corresponds to Jung's 'individuation' process. Though this model seems more fluid, it is not universal. Many clients get off before the last stop because 'Each stage . . . has something curiously final about it' (1929c, p. 68). Jung's four-stage blueprint thus remains a somewhat superficial exercise with limited application to the perplexities of in-depth, clinical work.

However, it should be noted that the final, 'transformation' stage above really involves the 'mutual transformation' of therapist and client (Jung, 1929c, p. 72). Therefore it is at this point that Searles' ideas can be compared with Jung's, and where Jung in a later work (1946) offers some detailed analysis of the mutual process. The 'mutual transformation' stage is another name for the transference process, discussed earlier in this chapter.

In describing the stages of transformation in therapy, Jung and Searles both use analogies and idiosyncratic perspectives. In Searles' format the transference is analogous to the early, mother–child relationship. He outlines the stages in developmental terms, not merely because he likes that metaphor but because the early warp is what is to be transformed by therapy. Searles' discussion of 'the "normal" and predictable overall course of psychotherapy' also relies heavily on 'the crucial role of feelings' in therapist and client (1961g, p. 523). The stages he outlines are actually feeling-stages.

Jung's chief transformation analogy is a true metaphor. He finds that the imagery of alchemy – the arcane, medieval chemistry that attempted to turn base metals into gold – 'coincides in the most remarkable way' with unconscious imagery arising at different stages of the transference process (Jung, 1946, p. 200). This is a long way from Searles' real-life, mother–child orientation. Yet it is consistent with Jung's hypothesis of an historical, collective unconscious. Since Jungian transformation has an archetypal dimension, it needs something more, or at least different, than a very personalized metaphor. Jung's focus is also on what is happening in the unconscious, as mediated by these symbols. Searles' emphasis is a little more on the interpersonal realm. Actually, both authors are interested in transformation of the unconscious but, put another way, Jung studies this through 'symbols' and Searles through therapist–client 'feelings.' However, Jung also delineates the feelings at different stages, thus creating some important parallels with Searles' model.

Searles outlines five stages, the first three of which correct and correspond 'in reverse' to the early mother–child failure that caused the client's illness (1961g, p. 523). Stage one is the *out of contact* stage, in which the client is autistically separated from the therapist's world and the therapist, accordingly, feels rather neutral in return. During the next stage of transference, *ambivalent symbiosis*, ego-boundaries collapse and therapist and client become emotionally enmeshed in a negative, often 'sticky' way (1961g, p. 523). The analyst's feelings oscillate rapidly and confusingly, in part because he is literally experiencing the client's feelings. Although the therapist at this point is the Bad Mother to the client, the client nevertheless may assume 'unparalleled importance in the therapist's life' (1961g, p. 533). *Preambivalent* or *therapeutic symbiosis* is the third stage, in which the therapist becomes Good Mother to the child-client, and vice versa. Both participants thrive in an atmosphere of mutual trust, love, and playfulness. This healing oneness cannot last forever, however, and either client or therapist will eventually instigate moves toward freedom, or the *resolution of symbiosis* stage. Though he feels great loss, now the therapist feels 'out of love' with the client and begins to challenge and in effect hold the client responsible for the continuance of his illness (1961g, p. 544). This process continues on into the *late stage*: the client now has some measure of object relations and can accept or reject identifications with past figures or the therapist.

In its most crucial dimension, Searles' model involves a mutual regression to a core stage, full symbiosis, that was never healthily experienced and never properly resolved. In later works (1970a, 1971, 1973a) Searles tends to combine stages two and three into a single *symbiosis* stage, basically because both are 'therapeutic' and also difficult to differentiate from each other (Searles, 1973a, p. 174). Stages four and five are also consolidated and become simply *individuation* (Searles, 1971). Stage one remains *out of contact* (*autism*), but Searles comes to see it as a defense against the therapeutic symbiosis (1970a, 1971). Clearly, Searles' model changes or loosens with deepening experience. His final sequence is flexible: either pathological symbiosis → autism → therapeutic symbiosis → individuation (1971) or autism → symbiosis → individuation (1970a). As previously noted (see Chapter 2), the last stage in Searles' theory, individuation, is the least well developed.

Jung's (1946) description through alchemical imagery of the transformation/transference process naturally has a very different flavor than Searles'. If Searles' mother–child symbiosis is, so to speak, one step removed from the therapist–client interaction, Jung's alchemical reference point is still farther away. His presentation is not grounded in a human relationship at all, but in a ritualistic, archaic science. Still, all this is in accord with Jung's view of the unconscious as a non-personal acquisition.

The sequence Jung outlines essentially boils down to five stages for which Jung uses alchemical terminology. Stage one in alchemical treatises is alternately called 'divisio,' 'solutio,' 'separatio' or 'putrefactio' (Jung, 1944, p. 230). The best word, for this book's purposes, is *separatio*, because this stage is characterized alchemically by a separation of the elements and therapeutically by a sometimes long period of 'foregoing preliminary talk' (Jung, 1946, p. 182). At a certain point, however, this preliminary discussion 'touches the unconscious and establishes the unconscious identity of doctor and patient' (1946, p. 183). This is the second or *nigredo* ('blackening') period, in which there is a boundaryless chaos and distrust as unconscious contents rebound back and forth between the participants. This unconscious therapist–client enmeshment deepens until a kind of static, psychic death occurs, a 'death' which is nevertheless alchemically symbolized by the union – *coniunctio* – of opposites in the unconscious (1946, p. 257). Stage three is one of a total but paradoxical unconsciousness, corresponding in its negative aspect to an inert state, but in its positive form to a marriage or 'conjunction.' This union in the unconscious is really pregnant with meaning, as evidenced by the next stage in which the 'divine child,' symbol of the Self, first appears (1946, p. 272). The newborn Self, though, is a little wet behind the ears and, in the alchemical imagery, ascends to heaven; hence this stage of transference calls for and is called *mundificatio* (purification). That is, the Self must be brought down to earth and so must the person who discovers this eternal Self. The successful completion of this task results in the fifth and final stage of total *albedo* ('whitening'), symbolized in alchemy by the hermaphroditic 'philosopher's son' or 'stone' (1946, p. 248).

Though it is easy to get lost in abstruse symbolism, particularly in Jung's version, a comparison of both theorists' models proves fruitful. The first transference developments, *out of contact* and *separatio*, are characterized in both theories by a certain 'apartness' of client, therapist and their respective unconsciouses. As previously noted, Searles views the client's autism as a repressive defense against a rising need to see the therapist-mother as 'the whole functional world' (1970a, p. 150). The client cannot yet tolerate the therapist's importance to him, and the therapist usually feels emotionally unengaged too.

Jung does not speak directly to the 'importance' issue in stage one – except by name ('separation' = unengaged) and especially by implication. For in his stage two, *nigredo*, the therapist finds that 'the case begins to "fascinate" him' and move him quite personally (Jung, 1946, p. 176). This view is only slightly different, in degree, from Searles' on the 'unparalleled importance' the client has for the therapist in *ambivalent symbiosis* (1961g, p. 533).

There are other close parallels in the authors' respective second stages. According to Searles, disappearing ego-boundaries make for 'complementary' identity between analyst and patient (1971, p. 134). Together the two participants form one rather tense, mutually hostile, 'whole' person. Similarly Jung describes *nigredo* as an unconscious identity, of a type characterized by mutual distrust and 'dangerous polar tensions' (1946, p. 187). For both theorists, though, the essential transference feature is a feeling of being lost in a chaotic intermingling. Within this confusing 'fog,' Jung notes that 'The elusive, deceptive, ever-changing content that possesses the patient like a demon now flits about from patient to doctor' (1946, pp. 187–8). This is very much like Searles' comment that in the sticky *ambivalent symbiosis* neither participant can tell whether thoughts or feelings are his own or the other person's (1961g, 1973a). The fusion is that complete.

Searles and Jung even show some commonality regarding a defensive, pseudo-mutuality that can occur around this stage or the next. Jung decries a kind of phony 'harmony' that may exist between client and therapist, making the differentiation of the

114

unconscious introjects difficult (1946, p. 187). Likewise Searles sometimes questions whether a purely unambivalent symbiosis can exist at all:

> There is no sure criterion by which we can know . . . whether we are involved in a genuinely preambivalent symbiosis with the patient, or rather in the predominantly paranoid symbiosis which is a defense against hatred. . . . A basically constructive, subjectively preambivalent symbiosis will be misused unconsciously from time to time, by both participants, to keep increments of particularly intense hostility out of awareness.
>
> (Searles, 1961g, p. 542)

Accordingly, Searles later combines the two stages into one *symbiosis* (1970a). However, he later goes on again to differentiate the non-therapeutic and therapeutic varieties (1971, 1973a, 1980).

At any rate, the third stages of *therapeutic symbiosis* and *coniunctio* also share some similarities. First, though, there is a seemingly vast difference. Searles' version portrays therapist and client engaged in a 'blissful oneness' or 'nirvana,' which has its 'prototype' in healthy mother–child interaction (1980, p. 106). Jung's third stage is the shadow of this: a total merger into an egoless state, but one that is characterized by a deathlike submersion into unconsciousness. Searles' is a playful loss of ego, while Jung's seems foreboding and energyless. Therefore, the partners in Searles' version are in no hurry to leave this stage. In contrast, therapist and client in Jung's model would probably prefer to leave this 'valley of the shadow' as soon as possible (1946, p. 198).

Nevertheless, similarities arise when the theorists' third stages are considered in terms of the overall process. In both instances, wholeness has been achieved – but it is an unconscious, undeveloped one. It is also a transitional one, a transitional stage rather than the finale of the transformation sequence. Searles suggests that *preambivalent symbiosis* provides 'the basis for renewed, and healthier, development of individuality' (1961g, p. 543). Likewise, Jung's *coniunctio* signifies death but also rebirth: the union in the unconscious results in a 'psychic pregnancy' (Jung, 1946, p. 255). Having achieved a necessary goal, both regressions now face forward. Searles' 'nirvana' and Jung's 'death' both imply unconsciousness; the next step is consciousness.

Consciousness demands two things that are represented by the theorists' fourth stages: differentiation and sacrifice. Jung's *mundificatio*, or 'purification,' is 'an attempt to discriminate the mixture,' particularly the mix of ego and newborn Self (1946, p. 293). The *coniunctio* has produced a touch of eternity, the 'divine child' or Self, which must not be annexed by the ego (or else one would consider oneself a god). Searles' *resolution of symbiosis* also involves a deflation of eternity, in the form of giving up the cherished, symbiotic oneness. Therapist and client are no longer 'one' but 'two,' and the therapist finds himself holding his client accountable for his behavior and illness. The doctor calls the patient down to earth, just as in Jung's parallel stage the doctor insists on the separation of the real man and the transcendent Self. For both theorists, eternity, once experienced, must be sacrificed in favor of adult consciousness and human life.

Jung's *albedo* and Searles' *late stage* have in common the fact that they both are really extensions of the fourth stage. As noted before, Searles in later works tends to combine his final stages into one essential *individuation* stage (1970a, 1971, 1973a). Similarly, Jung's *mundificatio* and *albedo* overlap: the 'purification' is part of the 'whitening' (Jung, 1946, p. 273). In addition, the ultimate goals of both men's fifth stages are never fully achieved. Perfect consciousness and individuation do not exist. Perhaps appropriately, the role of the therapist in stage five receives less attention than in earlier steps. Jung's therapist focus is strongest in the *nigredo* and *coniunctio* stages. Similarly, Searles confesses that he has yet to discover the definitive word on *individuation* (1980).

If Jung's alchemical model seems obscure, then it must be added that Searles' model is equally unpredictable: he keeps combining stages and changing their sequence. In the final analysis, both theorists strive for but do not achieve a consistent, systematic blueprint of the transformation process. In this they are quite similar and quite realistic.

Summary

Jung and Searles show much resemblance in their therapy goals. Rather than attempting to reverse pathology, they encourage a greater subjective awareness on the client's part, keynoted by the withdrawal of projections. Imagos are not only withdrawn but worked on, with Searles promoting their repair and Jung their amplification.

From the less technical perspective of the patient, both therapists' goal is the creation of a more fluid personality. In general terms, Searles and Jung promote the patient's establishment of a continuous or whole sense of identity. However, these wider goals are based on the fundamental process of imago-repair. The specific ends of therapy are met specifically in therapy, according to Searles and Jung, but ideally a therapeutic attitude should continue after termination. Therefore, both authors share the implicit goal for the client of developing an 'internal' therapist-imago.

The key to 'cure' rests dynamically on the analyst–patient relationship, though Jung cites other healing factors in less serious cases. An intense, emotional interaction between participants at an unconscious level is at the core of transference, according to both authors. Patient and therapist are involuntarily gripped and changed by an autonomous transformation process. This curative process specifically seems to rest on an exchange of 'healthy' and 'ill' components in each participant's personality. Searles in particular emphasizes that the therapist works on the client's psychopathology and vice versa, while Jung suggests that therapist and client focus on mutual, archetypal issues. Regardless, it seems to both writers that transference means transference of illness to the therapist. The end result, though Jung stresses the symbolic and Searles the interpersonal, is that both therapist and patient are 'in therapy.'

Jung and Searles agree that this combustible mix of personalities at conscious and unconscious levels requires an underlying framework in which to work. The basic, stabilizing structure for the transference is emotional, though an 'outer' frame of trust and containment in the therapist–client relationship seems to permit an 'inner' intermingling. For both authors, a maximally therapeutic environment is established in conjunction with the transference involvement.

While highlighting experiential rather than interpretive aspects of therapy, Searles and Jung also share a very favorable evaluation of work with unconscious fantasy. Jung's high opinion of symbolic fantasy contrasts slightly with Searles' interpersonal emphasis, though this may be an artifact of Searles' clientele. Related to this is Searles' focus on hallucinations as against Jung's

117

on dreams, yet their ways of working with each tend toward common ground.

When interpreting unconscious material, both theorists interpret often and expect mistakes. Yet they each interpret with a detailed awareness of the client's position and personality, though the particulars of their assessments are different. Jung's and Searles' attitudes toward 'resistance' also overlap. They both find the client's resistance appropriate rather than defensive. More so than Searles, Jung also seeks unconscious verification of the therapist's interpretations.

Jung and Searles differ most fundamentally on the content of their interpretations. Jung's assumption is that symbolism is archetypal and dynamic, whereas Searles looks more to static, regressive or defensive elements. Like Jung however, Searles ultimately emphasizes the accuracy and not the distortion in fantasy. Both theorists interpret fantasies, even sexual fantasies, in symbolic, compensatory or purposive ways. Their theories also share a 'subjective' approach in which fantasy refers to the fantasizer's personality. Jung and Searles are even alike in their contradictory statements about 'objective' interpretation. They show evidence of a theory/practice difference, preferring subjective interpretations in theory but making much use of objective ones in their clinical work.

Jung and Searles are equally pragmatic in their use of fantasy products as a measure of therapeutic progress. Jung also insists that symbolic contents have inherent, untranslatable meaning. Searles, while hoping clients will develop the capacity to fantasize, is more concerned with reality considerations than the reality of fantasy.

In terms of the stages of therapy, Searles and Jung differ superficially in that Jung offers some rudimentary, textbook outlines while Searles offers none. The theorists meet, though, when describing the five sub-stages of the transformative, transference interaction. They use different metaphors, mother and child (Searles) vs. alchemy (Jung), but frequently overlap regarding the emotions alive in the therapeutic situation.

5

THE THERAPIST

Chapter 3 discussed psychopathology, which by nature focuses on the patient. In Chapter 4 the psychotherapy process, in which both patient and therapist are involved, was the center of attention. Now the perspective again changes, and in this chapter the therapist becomes the focal point.

Of course, the work of the therapist was mentioned in some detail in the last chapter – that is, the kind of work and the kind of 'process' he is engaged in with the client. Certain 'rules' about therapist character or behavior, as hinted at by Jung and Searles, became evident in the discussion: the therapist is emotionally involved, pathologically inclined, reliant on his unconscious, sometimes confused, and so on. In this chapter these dimensions and others not directly apparent in the 'process' chapter will be elucidated and explored. The therapist's role and personality will here be isolated and analyzed more specifically.

Much as the transition between Chapters 3 and 4 involved a movement into the therapy process from psychopathology, so this chapter involves a slight movement out of the process itself. This chapter even moves to a point somewhat outside of the therapist: paradoxically, it moves away in order to view the therapist more closely. It is like a certain type of supervisory session, focusing on the therapy but mostly on the therapist. What is the therapist's role, and what is the nature and effect (on him) of his participation in therapy? These are some of the questions, and they lead to broader questions: why does one become a therapist or stay one, and what sort of *person* is the therapist?

Thus, this chapter focuses on the therapist both in and out of the session. With pathology, process and cure dynamics discussed, the shift in this chapter is to a more distant, almost retrospective view. But one that looks to the future.

Personality as technique

In discussing the dynamics of cure in Chapter 4, the unconscious interchange of 'sick' and 'well' components between analyst and patient was postulated as a primary factor. Such an intermingling is clearly not a matter of 'technique,' at least not in the usual 'applied' sense of the word. It is certainly not a conscious process either, nor one that could be learned from a textbook.

But while it is not and could not be a technique, it is clear that the therapist's 'personality' as a whole is the chief instrument at his disposal. Jung summarizes this in this way: 'We have learned to place in the foreground the personality of the doctor himself as a curative or harmful factor. . . . The crucial thing is no longer the medical diploma, but the human quality' (1929c, pp. 74–5). Searles similarly states that 'countertransference,' including the therapist's 'personality and especially his sense of identity,' are 'of the greatest and most reliable research and therapeutic value' (1975b, p. 376).

Thus personality *is* a sort of technique after all, according to Searles and Jung. More precisely, the therapist 'uses' his personal reactions as a primary technique. This is somewhat ironic in that the point of proper technique is usually to avoid the foibles of unstandardized, unscientific subjectivity. Yet Jung's and Searles' 'technique' promotes just that.

However, both theorists suggest a refinement of the therapist's personality, in order that he may then successfully use it. The simple employment of personal reactions would be too cavalier. As Jung says, 'If the wrong man uses the right means, the right means work in the wrong way. . . . Everything depends on the man and little or nothing on the method' (1929b, p. 83). By the same token, Searles believes that there is danger in an analyst's using countertransference as technique 'without having first acquired the requisite personal acquaintance with his own unconscious and the requisite degree of clinical experience' (1973c, p. 359).

These warnings bring up the matter of 'how' the therapist can perfect his personality for technical use. The first and most important way is through his own personal analysis. Searles repeatedly stresses that a training analysis is vital, since it provides the therapist with more accurate access to, though not elimination of, his own unconscious feeling processes, the core of countertransference (1949/79, 1973c, 1975b). Jung's parallel emphasis is evidenced by his insistence, later adopted by psychoanalysis in general, that all analysts be psychoanalyzed (1929c, 1935b, 1946; see also Ellenberger, 1970). Like Searles, Jung believes that the therapist's unconscious will not thereby be emptied, but at least his reactions to the client will be less tainted by his own projections. As Jung puts it, 'The doctor himself must have clean hands' (1935b, p. 13).

While the therapist polishes his personality through personal analysis, he also does so by doing analysis later. That is, he refines his technique continuously through practice. This relates to Searles' above comment about 'clinical experience.' It also follows logically from the fact (see Chapter 4) that therapist and client are *both* 'in analysis.' In a sense, then, the therapist 'uses' the client to develop his own subjective skills – for the benefit of that same client and future clients.

The results of these ongoing attempts by the therapist at perfecting his own personality as a therapeutic tool take a particular form. What he is really developing is a subjectivity that he can trust. Stated in different terms, what he learns to do is not only understand but *rely* on his emotions as accurate indicators of an interpersonal or even intrapsychic situation (in the patient). What is implied in this self-trusting attitude is a wider perspective, namely, that emotions and feeling-life are valuable. Affects are sometimes thought to be 'wrong' or distasteful, yet the analyst's point of view declares that they are 'right.' Rather than be avoided, they should be prized for their informative value, just as the therapist so uses them in therapy. The apparent subjectivity of feelings is thereby really an objectivity. Furthermore, a client could obviously have no better model for engaging his emotional life than the therapist who does likewise in his dealings with that client.

If there is one thing that characterizes the therapist, then, it is this valuing of affectivity *per se*. In Chapter 2 it was noted that, according to Jung and Searles, emotion is the basis of personality. In Chapter 3 it was cited as the dynamic basis of therapy. Here it appears as a prime trait in the hierarchical value system of the therapist.

The style of the therapist

Related to this high evaluation of feelings is the therapist's corresponding devaluation of 'neutrality' as a therapeutic or interpersonal stance. Neutrality is often equated with objectivity, and a common desideratum is that the analyst not influence the apparently dependent client. For Jung and Searles, however, the mutual influence of therapist and client is unavoidable *and* desirable (see Chapter 4): the therapist cannot be neutral. Says Jung, 'Despite all rational safeguards, the patient does attempt to assimilate the analyst's personality. . . . Patients read the analyst's character intuitively' (1914, p. 26). Searles states in even stronger language that a pseudo-'mature,' emotionless attitude 'would require that a therapist of integrity be either obsessive or schizoid' (1973c, pp. 362–3). Searles later adds that the traditional idea 'that the analyst is not at all a real person to the patient simply will not do' (1975a, p. 458).

Searles and Jung do not imply, though, that the impossibility of pure neutrality means the therapist should ride roughshod over the client. They merely believe that therapist neutrality cannot be assumed or established at the outset of therapy – a neutral 'technique' by no means guarantees neutrality. Searles in fact suggests that a relative neutrality toward a client is *achieved* during the course of therapy with each client (1976a). Nor does Jung banish neutrality totally: 'It is certainly very laudable in a doctor to try to be as objective and impersonal as possible and to refrain from meddling with the psychology of his patient like an overzealous savior' (1934b, pp. 159–60). However, Jung drily adds:

> But if this is carried to artificial lengths it has unfortunate consequences. The doctor will find that he cannot overstep the bounds of naturalness with impunity. Otherwise he would be setting a bad example to his patient, who certainly did not get ill from an excess of naturalness.
>
> (Jung, 1934b, p. 160)

Here again, 'natural' rather than 'neutral' reactions in the analyst are valued.

Linked to the analyst's well-trained, well-analyzed subjectivity is another personality trait, expressiveness. Attending to his emotions does not necessarily imply that the therapist needs to

122

express them. He may 'feel' richly, use his personality vividly, yet keep all this hidden or unshared. But for Jung and Searles therapeutic anonymity is almost as unnecessary as the pretension to neutrality. The therapist's experience of affect and the use of his personality in relation to the client seem to imply at least some expression thereof. Jung, even more so than Searles, believes in spontaneity, as implied in the remarks above about the therapist's 'naturalness.' Earlier, too, Jung was quoted as saying, 'I expose myself completely and react with no restriction' (1935a, p. 139).[1] According to Jung such reactions give patients 'orientation' to reality, and to the effects of their own personalities on others (1935a, p. 139). Along this latter dimension, Searles cogently remarks that almost all clients are desperately trying 'to prove to themselves that they can have an emotional effect on other persons' (1949/79, p. 182). Anonymity in the therapist cripples these attempts, installing the therapist in transference as the 'schizoid' (1949/79, p. 183) or 'omnipotent' parent (1976b, p. 587) whose strivings the client sadistically foils by being mentally ill. Therefore, Searles' conclusion on expressiveness is very much like Jung's:

> Outer reality for the patient during the analytic session consists most immediately in the person of the analyst and in what the analyst is feeling and thinking. I have seldom found that a patient reacts in any lastingly traumatized way to my communicating to him, for example, the feelings or fantasies I find myself experiencing in response to him.
>
> (Searles, 1973b, p. 280)

Just as clients are encouraged to de-repress emotions, so the therapist's use of his subjective self demands true expression rather than repression. Such usage also demands *accurate* expression; in other words, the therapist must be able to readily identify the subjective component to be used and expressed. This raises the overall issue of the therapist's self-awareness, another positive personality trait. For Jung and Searles, the therapist's ability to recognize and articulate his subjectivity forms a complement to the very existence of that subjectivity.

Self-awareness in the therapist does not derive necessarily from superior intelligence (in the usual sense). Instead it consists of an easy, conscious access to countertransference states, coupled with a basically non-defensive attitude toward them. These two aspects of self-awareness may really amount to the same thing.

As pointed out in Chapter 4, the therapist typically has a quicker access than the client to feelings. Aside from his lengthy training and training analysis, what gives the therapist this speedier consciousness is a practiced intuition. Intuition, as a sort of non-cognitive cognition, is in fact an appropriate means of ascertaining feelings. Emotional life, for Jung and Searles, does not respond to logic. Feelings are less liable to be 'thought' out or derived than 'sensed,' rather vaguely – that is, intuitively.

Jung even points out the linguistic parallels between feeling and intuition: intuition occurs when one 'gets a feeling,' or hunch, that something will happen (1935a, p. 14). At any rate, both Searles (1961b) and Jung (1945) stress the therapist's use of his intuitive faculty. A highly developed intuition not only provides access to his own and the client's unconscious, but it also enables the therapist to know *when* to mention or interpret feelings. Searles puts this most succinctly while citing the 'necessity' of the therapist's 'inner freedom to experience' feelings and fantasies about the patient:

> Only his therapeutic intuition, grounded in his accumulating clinical experience, can best instruct him when it is timely and useful – and when, on the other hand, it is ill timed and injudicious – to *express* these inner experiences.
>
> (Searles, 1973a, p. 179)

Again, a certain 'sixth sense' serves the therapist well.

The other aspect of self-awareness, a non-defensive attitude, essentially arises from the therapist's personal analysis. This goal of therapy is desirable for therapist as 'client,' as it is for any client. Actually, the therapist is not exactly undefended or defenseless. It is evident from Jung's (1946, p. 172) confession that he prefers a 'mild transference' or Searles' (1967b, p. 73) statements about the necessity of a full 'armamentarium' against his uniformly sadistic clients, that the therapist is not without defenses. Likewise, the authors' visions of therapy as 'ordeal' (Jung, 1951b, p. 116) or 'hell' (Searles, 1976b, p. 587) would necessitate some level of defensiveness in any but a superhuman therapist. In terms of defenses, what Jung and Searles have in mind is not a naïve 'no defenses' attitude, but a struggle and recognition with them as they arise. The therapist's self-awareness consists of intuitions and knowledge not only about his feelings *per se* but about his reluctances or hesitations – his fears about those feelings.

The analyst therefore may be said to have a reluctant honesty about himself. In the battle of truth vs. falsehood, he grudgingly chooses truth, or tries to. Indeed, this is what he encourages the client to do as well. And as this attitude of 'honesty above all' grows habitual in the therapist, it shapes the ways he views and approaches the client, not to mention life in general.

The particular form this general honesty takes is reflected in the therapist's attitude toward 'helping' clients. In lieu of a helpful (in the sense of 'loving' or 'caring') attitude, the therapist adopts a truthful one. As Searles points out, prevailing cultural, medical and psychoanalytic norms seem to call for a dedicated, ever-solicitous response to long-suffering clients by people in the helping professions (1966a). However, this kind of maternal, 'Christian' ideal is not one that Jung and Searles espouse. For instance, Jung in a letter criticizes a fellow therapist in these terms:

> You *wanted* to help, which is an encroachment upon the will of others. Your attitude ought to be that of one who offers an opportunity that can be taken or rejected. Otherwise you are most likely to get into trouble. It is so because man is not fundamentally good, almost half of him is a devil.
>
> (Jung, 1973b, p. 84)

Searles similarly suggests that the therapist's unstinting 'devotion' to saving the hapless client is patronizing, defensive and, in the final analysis, 'a lie' (1967b, p. 87).

Both theorists take this characteristic even farther by suggesting that the therapist himself must sometimes be, to use Jung's word, a sort of 'devil.' That is, he must be able to feel and even act bluntly and harshly with his honesty. As Jung states:

> Some people deserve that you should not be kind. When you give to them, you are warming yourself with the thought of your wonderful kindness, but you are wronging them, leading them further into error. So you need a certain amount of cruelty.
>
> (Jung, 1976, p. 272)

Searles' parallel comment is:

> For far too long we have failed to see that the analyst, not only for the sake of his own mental hygiene but also to work effectively as an analyst, must be free to think and

125

feel critically, judgmentally, and, not at all seldom, condemningly.

(Searles, 1966a, p. 30)

In short, the therapist need not 'love' his clients at all times. He may critically evaluate their actions, and share these judgments – just as if the client were what he actually is, a human being.

This sometimes callous attitude in the therapist has a corollary aspect that tempers his relations with the client. Given his potential bluntness, the therapist might be expected to guide the patient in his daily life. Instead, Searles and Jung suggest a nondirective stance. Tied to this is a more fundamental feeling that the client's illness and life are ultimately the client's own responsibility. Searles states adamantly that the final *choice* to be sick or sane lies with the client (1961g, 1967b, 1976b). Important in this regard is the therapist's allowing the patient to have this choice, which the therapist does by gradually becoming able to tolerate the possibility of the patient's *never* recovering (Searles, 1976b, p. 597). Thus the therapist renounces his curative dedication.

In terms also of the 'past,' or origin, of the illness, Searles ultimately holds the client accountable for his identifications with his parents, however pathological the latter were in themselves (1975b). His summary conclusion cites the patient and frees the therapist:

A dozen years ago I reached the conviction that it is folly to set out to rescue the patient from the dragon of schizophrenia: the patient is both the maiden in the dragon's grip, and the dragon itself. The dragon is the patient's resistance to becoming 'sane' – resistance which shows itself as a tenacious and savage hostility to the therapist's efforts.

(Searles, 1967b, p. 75)

Compared to Searles, Jung deems the client less personally responsible for his introjects (because they are mostly impersonal archetypes) or for the 'past' (at least in the case of children, see Chapter 3). However, Jung does criticize the patient (and/or the therapist) who uses the past as an excuse for avoiding the tasks of the present: 'It is only in today, not in our yesterdays, that the neurosis can be "cured"' (1934b, p. 171). Delving overlong into historical derivations is subterfuge.

Similarly, whatever attempts the client does make, through therapy or otherwise, to deal with the 'present' should not be interfered with by the therapist. Even with misguided efforts, Jung maintains an essentially nondirective position:

> The doctor should not strive to heal at all costs. One has to be exceedingly careful not to impose one's own will and conviction on the patient. We have to give him a certain amount of freedom. You can't wrest people away from their fate. . . . Sometimes it is really a question whether you are allowed to rescue a man from a fate he must undergo for the sake of further development.
>
> (Jung, 1935a, p. 131)

Because it is his own life, the patient must learn to succeed or fail in his own way. Then his life is really 'his.' For Jung as with Searles, final responsibility is turned over to the client, even if the therapist senses potential failure or complication.

The nondirective therapist viewpoint chosen by both theorists does not rest simply on callousness nor on an ethic of individual freedom and personal responsibility. Also relevant is a certain practicality. Searles and Jung believe that the therapist probably cannot, as well as should not, direct the client's life. Often the client will just not respond to such attempts, anyway. As Searles notes, one of the client's chief sources of 'sadistic gratification' is to unconsciously thwart the best intentions of parents and therapists (1975b, p. 378). The directive therapist sets himself up for frustration and failure. In a more conscious way, the client may simply reject or ignore directions from the therapist, much as he resists improper interpretations (Searles, 1970a; Jung, 1951b).

The personality of the therapist

So far, it appears that the therapist can use his subjectivity freely – as long as he knows what his feelings actually are. He may hate or criticize the client, let him 'go to hell in his own way.' Nevertheless, if the more charitable end of the spectrum seems to be downplayed by Searles and Jung, it is only a temporary oversight. For both theorists include it in their inventory of therapist traits. Searles' descriptions of 'full' or 'therapeutic symbiosis' involve a mutually adoring, joyful oneness (1961g, p. 537). In an earlier work Searles also says that

... with every one of my patients who has progressed to, or very far towards, a thoroughgoing analytic cure, I have experienced romantic and erotic desires to marry, and fantasies of being married to, the patient.

(Searles, 1959b, p. 284)

Searles furthermore concludes that, of all the feelings the therapist has toward the client, hate is ultimately 'subsidiary to' or 'dissolves into' love (1965b, p. 24). Jung's thoughts on the therapist's affectionate feelings for clients, as noted earlier, revolve around love as a compensation for conscious distance between them. That the therapist's emotional experience may include romantic feelings is distinctly and indubitably evidenced by the fact that Jung had affairs with one, and possibly two, of his patients, apparently after therapy (Hannah, 1976; Carotenuto, 1982).

'Falling in love' with patients may be the exception rather than the rule, but a non-eroticized type of caring or concern is a basic therapist quality, according to Searles and Jung. The specific form this takes is 'empathy.' As opposed to the nurturing, solicitous trait, criticized above, that might be called 'sympathy,' empathy involves a true identification with the client. At a deep level the therapist shares the client's feelings from the latter's point of view, insofar as that is possible. Although Jung and Searles champion the therapist's freedom to be critical of the client, the therapist's critical faculty is temporarily suspended during empathic moments. Jung puts it well: 'If the doctor wants to guide another, or even accompany him a step of the way, he must *feel* with that person's psyche. He never feels it when he passes judgment' (1973a, p. 90).

Searles, who works with the most chronically schizophrenic patients imaginable, still tries 'to share the patient's *feelings about* the world as he perceives it, rather than challenge the accuracy of his perceptual world itself.... I try largely to put aside my own view of reality' (1967a, p. 23). Following this empathic engagement, the therapist may then attempt to share, confront or insist on the 'differences between *his* world and ours' (Searles, 1967a). Thus according to both Jung and Searles, the therapist's empathic efforts come first, then his more natural, even critical reactions may follow. This sequence, of course, corresponds to the natural sequence of listening/responding inherent in any conversation, only at a more genuine, hopefully therapeutic level. Empathy really has to do with a deep involvement in the 'listening process.'

Searles and Jung even describe the mechanism of empathy in the same way. Searles believes that empathy with a client's past requires that the therapist have parallel experiences in his own developmental history (1978, p. 73). The degree of congruence (how similar?) is not detailed by Searles – it is probable that he means the therapist must have had roughly equal emotional conflicts or deprivations, rather than exactly the same life 'happenings.' Clearly, Searles assumes some universality of human experience and some flexibility in how precise the 'fit' must be for empathy to occur. Jung explains the dynamics of empathy in almost precisely the same way, leaving out only the 'developmental' aspect. Empathy is an 'active' process, says Jung, which

... brings the object into intimate relation with the subject. In order to establish this relationship, the subject detaches a content – a feeling, for instance – from himself, lodges it in the object, thereby animating it, and in this way draws the object into the sphere of the subject.

(Jung, 1921, p. 458)

Therefore Searles and Jung agree not only on the necessity of empathy in the therapist, but on the sequence and source of the empathic process.

If it is his own experience that provides the therapist with his empathic capabilities, another characteristic of his personality also comes to light. Rather than being a 'selfless' helper of others, the therapist is more or less intensely preoccupied with *himself.* All the self-awareness and self-reference involved in the therapy process makes him 'selfish,' in a certain literal sense of that word. From a negative viewpoint he might be seen as narcissistic or egocentric. On the other hand, the therapist so criticized might reply that his intense self-interest is in the best interests of his clients. Jung even suggests that individual self-knowledge is the first step toward solving the sociopolitical problems of mankind (1928a, 1957). Politics aside, in Searles' and Jung's view it is evident that the therapist puts his ability for self-analysis at the service of others. The therapist is an expert at paying attention to himself.

The therapist actually puts more than just his positive narcissism in the hands of the client. He turns himself, his conscious and unconscious person, over to the client to, in effect, be 'used.' Earlier it was suggested that the therapist in effect utilizes the client to 'practice' on; now it seems that the client similarly uses the therapist (if possible[2]). And he pays him for it. While the therapist is not exactly a psychological 'prostitute,' he does allow and encourage the client to thus engage him. And he will be used, as Searles has noted, as a vehicle for the integration of all the patient's feelings, from nonhuman to godlike (1976a).

What enables the therapist to be so used is a trait of 'permeability' in his personality. Rather than being rigidly defined, his ego-boundaries are more amoeboid; the barriers shrink and expand. And this flexibility applies in two directions: the analyst seems to be particularly 'open' to clients *and* to his own unconscious. The therapist (like the client, incidentally) is easily moved by either internal or external affective stimuli. Searles, of course, places special emphasis on being affected by people, though this also means being affected by the other's unconscious processes as well as conscious ones. He states that he (and by extension the Searlesian therapist) is 'a very symbiotically oriented person' – so much so that he must be 'reclusive' to avoid constantly 'surrendering' his personality to the other person (Searles, 1980, p. 79). Jung's focus is slightly more on the therapist's private relationship to his intrapsychic realm, what he calls 'the confrontation with the unconscious' (1961b, p. 170). Jung himself was prone to visions and other paranormal phenomena. However, he notes that the client's unconscious processes invoke parallel archetypes in the therapist (Jung, 1946). So there is an interpersonal dimension to Jung's permeability as well.

This proneness to interpersonal or intrapsychic penetration is related to the 'non-defensiveness' mentioned earlier in this chapter. From the above, it becomes clear that the therapist is 'undefended' less by choice than by disposition. His ego-boundaries are inherently 'loose.' At a deeper level this also explains why self-awareness is an important attribute of the therapist: it is a necessity for his well-being.

Thus empathy in the therapist arises from his innate permeability and (over-?)sensitivities. The therapist seems to be a natural empathizer. He also seems to have a particular interest and relationship to emotional suffering, as reflected in his choice of profession. Empathy, as envisioned by Searles and Jung, demands a subjective identification through personal experience with the other person. Especially in psychotherapy the type of personal experience most often called upon is suffering. For, as Jung (1943a) and Searles (1967a) point out, it is that which the client has most avoided.

What turns out to be the therapist's preoccupation or even fascination with suffering does not derive just from empathic demands or some sort of quasi-voyeuristic curiosity. The implication in Searles' and Jung's writings is that the therapist has a special interest in suffering – his own. Chances are it was his personal sufferings that led him to the work, rather than vice versa. Even if he were not a doctor, he would probably be involved in the issues of suffering and healing.

This is not to envision the analyst as martyr or masochist. However, running through both Jung's and Searles' theories is a sense of the sobering dimensions of life, with which the therapist deals daily and to which he is resigned. Jung states:

> Life demands for its completion and fulfillment a balance between joy and sorrow. But because suffering is positively disagreeable, people naturally prefer not to ponder how much fear and sorrow fall to the lot of man. . . . Happiness is poisoned if the measure of suffering has not been fulfilled.
>
> (Jung, 1943a, p. 81)

Jung later goes on to speak of the 'fateful disposition' which leads the therapist to seek out this sort of profession (1946, p. 177). Similarly, he recommends that the therapist-to-be will learn his trade not from books but 'in the horrors of prisons, lunatic asylums and hospitals, in drab suburban pubs, in brothels and gambling hells' – the shadow side of life (Jung, 1912, p. 247).

Searles also takes up existential aspects of suffering in his discussions on life-changes (1961d), and death (1961f). In terms of the therapist, Searles' work is laced with examples of the quality and quantity of his own despair. His description of a taxi ride to the airport is typical:

> I was seized by an urge to leap from the cab and hurl myself off the bridge. . . . I simply could not face returning to my usual life in Washington, and the reason I found it intolerable to face was that I felt so shamefully and desperately unable 'simply' to face the living out of my life, the growing old and dying, the commonest, most everyday thing.
>
> (Searles, 1972b, p. 236)

As previously noted, Searles also mentions that the analyst often suffers more than his clients, who presumably are in rather severe, conscious or unconscious, anguish (1967b, 1976a).

For the therapist, then, life seems to involve a certain amount of suffering. He might be said to have a tragic sense of life, a sense which is no doubt reinforced by his working with patients. They help perpetuate this sense of things, not only through their pathologized lives and empathic demands, but through the fact that they often do not change very much or 'get well.' Doing therapy may not provide rewards commensurate with the degree of suffering it entails. Searles for instance notes that therapists 'do work that is neither tangible nor, in the usual sense of the term, completable' (1966a, p. 29). Therefore the work is inherently unsatisfactory and guilt-provoking. Jung likewise remarks on the unfinished quality of individuation, the goal of therapy: 'The united personality will never quite lose the painful sense of innate discord. . . . The goal is important only as an idea; the essential thing is the opus' (1946, p. 200). Also relevant is Jung's belief that crucial problems in life are fundamentally insoluble in any finalized sense (1929b, 1931c).

In every way the therapist leads a life in which suffering and failure are the 'way to be.' From one perspective, this makes him a sort of modern-age, existential hero, enduring and battling the ravages of an absurd world. On the other hand, many would view such a preoccupation as 'strange.' This is the 'therapists are crazy' school. Either way, what does become evident is that the therapist takes a position somewhat outside of the societal mainstream and conventional attitudes. Especially as portrayed by Searles and Jung, the therapist values and embodies independent or creative thought and action (much as he encourages autonomy for his clients).

Thus Searles' work has led him at times to seriously question 'whether sanity or psychosis is the more desirable mode of existence' (1976b, p. 590). He is not kidding. He cites the many gratifications of severe illness and suggests that the therapist might well be envious of them and envious, therefore, of the patient's psychosis. In another place Searles makes it plain that the viewpoints of psychotic individuals, who have necessarily been 'living on the sidelines of humanity,' can be enriching, provocative and often correct critiques of 'normal' life (1966a, p. 26). In like fashion, Jung frequently suggests that many clients are ill because they are too normal or too well-adapted (1929c, 1935b). He further says that his form of therapy takes up where 'rational' therapy leaves off (Jung, 1931f, p. 41) and involves an 'irrationalization of its [therapy's] aims' (Jung, 1935b, p. 26). Thus both analysts turn conventional attitudes on normality and rationality upside down. Overall, it may be said that the therapist in their systems is neither 'heroic' nor 'strange,' but he is definitely 'different.'

Thus far it appears that the therapist, 'the healer of souls,' is: subjective and emotional, intentionally un-'helpful' at times, vulnerable, not-so-normal, self-concerned, and so on. In many ways, in fact, he sounds just like a client. Despite the lengthy personal analysis prescribed by Searles and Jung, the therapist has evidently not been 'cured.'

Therefore it becomes clear that the therapist is not necessarily superior to the client. The notion of the therapist as an 'authority' to some extent holds true, but his expertise does not consist of any fundamental superiority of personality. He is perhaps quicker and more experienced with his self-awareness, less defensive by nature and training than the client, more empathic – that is what his 'health' consists of. He has a better relationship to his Self, or self.

Jung makes it clear, however, that any pretensions to being better than the 'so-called patient' must soon be abandoned: 'I do not know which is more difficult: to accumulate a wide knowledge or to renounce one's professional authority' (1935b, p. 18). If not given up, a sense of superiority may soon be ground down in the transference process. The related idea that the client is weak and the therapist strong also receives a critical review from Searles, who states, 'My feeling-orientation in starting to work with any schizophrenic patient is devoid of any simple assumption that I am stronger than he' (1976b, p. 585). Similarly, Jung remarks that in psychotherapy the 'stronger and more stable personality will decide the final issue,' but he notes that the 'stronger' one may not always be the therapist (1929c, p. 72).

The client's personality in fact may be superior in more than a general sense. Jung specifies that the client may possess greater 'intelligence, sensibility, range and depth' than the analyst (1935b, p. 10). Searles also suggests that certain clients may be 'more intelligent and creative and even in important respects more emotionally healthy' (1967a, p. 26).

The idea of the therapist as 'superior' is thus explicitly rejected by Searles and Jung. It is evidently a fantasy, and not just one promoted by the general societal belief that doctors lead some sort of elite existence. The fantasy is also played up by client and therapist both. The low self-esteem and helplessness that bring a client to treatment also activate a wishful or compensatory hope for a superior (parental or divine) helper. This elevated image may be projected onto the analyst. As postulated by Searles and Jung (see Chapter 2), projections are infectious, being part illusion but also part reality. The therapist is, after all, a helper, but he is not necessarily a 'better' human being than the client.

However, the narcissistic feeling of inherent superiority may prove tempting. Searles confides that the therapist's own fantasies not just of superiority but of 'omnipotence' are readily constellated (1966a, 1967b). Ironically, the more ill the client the greater the therapist's fantasy that, as Searles says,

> all his fondest dreams will materialize, one day, out of that unformed chaos over there – over there in the patient. . . . There are no discernible limits upon what future growth, with its wondrous possibilities for ego differentiation and integration, may bring.
>
> (Searles, 1976b, p. 586)

The sky is the limit for the omnipotent analyst. In the same ironic tone, Jung describes the effects of clients' 'savior' projections on the therapist:

> Of course the analyst will say, 'What nonsense! This is just morbid. It is a hysterical exaggeration.' Yet – it tickles him; it is just too nice. . . . So he begins to feel, 'If there are saviors, well, perhaps it is just possible that I am one.'
>
> (Jung, 1935a, p. 153)

Thus both theorists deflate any pretensions to grandiosity on the part of the therapist.

Nevertheless, there is one concession to delusions of grandeur that both Searles and Jung make. While struggling not to become overly inflated himself by the projection, the therapist must still in some way *receive* the projection. As mentioned in earlier chapters, the projected imagos may represent unconscious, undeveloped aspects of the client's personality, in this case positive ones needing integration rather than destruction. Jung notes, 'If a patient projects the savior complex onto you, for instance, you have to give back to him nothing less than the savior – whatever that means' (1935a, p. 152). The way to do this is not fully explained by Jung; apparently therapist and client must endure the 'transference deadlock' and follow the unconscious fantasy farther (Jung, 1928a, p. 131). Searles suggests, a little more specifically, 'What the patient requires is not omnipotence-in-action but, rather, the acceptance of the *patient's feelings of adoration*' (1962c, p. 623).[3] So the therapist must allow himself, perhaps temporarily, to be that 'adorable,' and must have in addition enough intact self-esteem to really feel that way. Perhaps what is involved here *is* a temporary experience of one's omnipotent feelings, at the behest and service of the patient.

Therapist/client

It was noted earlier that the therapist is basically nondirective in Jung's and Searles' systems, turning over responsibility for the client's life to the client. The therapist's manifest lack of superiority, coupled with his occasional inferiority *vis-à-vis* the client, implies a still greater sense of humility with regard to 'responsibility.' The therapist is really in no position to offer superior advice, according to Searles and Jung. Yet he does bear a heavy responsibility of a certain type. Because of the complex nature of the therapist/client interaction, consisting of a deep interchange of personality components (see Chapter 4), the patient becomes dependent on the analyst in more than the usual sense. The therapist's personality provides not only the means for doing therapy; it also sets the *limits* on how far the therapy may progress.

Jung states the matter directly: 'An analyst can help his patient just so far as he himself has gone and not a step further' (1937, p. 330). Therapy reaches an impasse at precisely the point 'where the analyst could make no further progress with himself' (1937, p. 330). At times Jung describes these limits as a function of 'how far the analyst has been analyzed himself' (1913, p. 198) but at other times the therapist's extra-therapy 'moral development' (1914, p. 260) is the key. Alternatively, the therapist must 'bring such passion for truth to the work that he can analyze himself through his patient' (Jung, 1928c, p. 137). Thus in Jung's view, the self-understandings of various sorts (highlighted in this chapter) define the parameters of therapeutic effectiveness.

Searles also believes that, if therapy stalls,

> the limitation tends rather to be in the analyst. The question is whether the analyst can achieve somehow the self-knowledge to become able to endure, and even enjoy, the transference positions into which largely unconscious forces within the schizophrenic patient tend to place him.
>
> (Searles, 1976b, p. 592)

As with Jung, the necessary 'self-knowledge' results from the therapist's personal analysis, providing as it does 'ready access' to the feelings against which the client is heavily defended (Searles, 1975b, p. 373). And Searles, even more than Jung, details the self-understandings the therapist comes to during and as a result of his everyday work. While Jung (1946, p. 178) states in a general way that most cases involve 'pioneer work' by the therapist (i.e., new understandings), Searles provides the specifics. As previously mentioned, in the transition out of 'therapeutic symbiosis' into 'individuation' it may be the therapist who is not ready to move (Searles, 1961g). Similarly, the client may be free to relinquish his 'illness' only after the therapist, who may be heavily invested in it, is able to (Searles, 1977b, p. 497). Or the therapist may need to come to grips with the client's 'maternal significance' to him (the therapist) before the client can do likewise (Searles, 1973c, p. 361). At all these junctures the client is, in effect, waiting for the therapist to understand his own unconscious reactions to the client (his countertransference).

Searles' above comments, as well as his notion of the patient as the analyst's therapist (Searles, 1975a), imply not only that the client can progress only as far as the therapist but that the client may have progressed farther. This is related to earlier quoted statements on the client's possession of capacities superior to the therapist's (intelligence, depth, etc.). But while Searles (in detail) and Jung (in passing) make it plain that the client can be farther along in therapy than the therapist, it is not necessarily true that the therapist has been as deeply ill as the client was outside of therapy. For all his 'patient'-vectors, 'hooks' and 'reality nuclei,' the doctor cannot have had precisely the same experience.

Whether the patient's and therapist's pathological experience must be exactly parallel is not the issue. The point is simply that the 'as far as' postulate regarding the limits of treatment progress has some 'limits.' Both Jung (1961b, p. 176) and Searles (1980,

p. 12) themselves admit that they have worried for their sanity or been close, for instance, to psychosis. But if there is a therapist characteristic that could be discerned in this, it might be that the therapist should have had some contact, perhaps an actual crisis but at least a personal 'brush,' with the illnesses he purports to empathize with. In other words he needs some sort of vivid experience of the reality of the unconscious. Searles and Jung are alike and interesting in the extent to which they encourage 'mutuality' with the client. Yet despite their 'loose boundaries,' they would have to agree that the therapist can be effective without having past experiences perfectly congruent with the client's.

In the final analysis, the therapist cannot pretend he has 'been there before,' any more than he can pretend to be innately superior, never inferior, always loving or always effective. The patient ultimately will find him out, because, as Jung says, 'Nothing is finer than the empathy of a neurotic' (1914, p. 277). Searles also notes the 'powerfully incisive accuracy' of clients' perceptual abilities and intuition (1967a, p. 23). All these points add up to a therapist quality that is learned if not initially given – humility. Try as he might, the therapist simply has no cause for grandiosity: he cannot stand above the process, the client or his own inferiorities.

A related idea (or consequence) is that the therapist must discover, at a genuine level, a fundamental sense of equality with his clients. This is not a given, either, but is earned over time. The analyst/patient encounter in Searles' and Jung's systems is largely stripped of 'normal' social considerations. The therapist must himself be comfortable with this, just as he encourages the client to be. Outer roles – like 'doctor' or 'patient' – diminish 'inside' therapy, such that a true, person-to-person engagement occurs. In Jung's words, 'The patient confronts the doctor upon equal terms' (1928c, p. 137). Searles characterizes this basic parity under the term 'reality-relatedness' (1961a, p. 378; 1961g, p. 556). In fact for him the 'real' feelings continuously evolving between therapist and client often precede and catalyze further transference developments.

The therapist has much cause for humility and much linkage, therefore, with the client. According to our theorists, the therapist's inferiority is often manifest and his equality with his client is most desirable. From an external vantage point, the therapist may appear 'healthier,' if only because he has probably never been as ill as the client. And even from the internal, private perspective – therapy viewing itself – the therapist must have some superior resources (Jung, 1946; Searles, 1976a). Part of the therapist's job – and a personal attitude, accordingly – is the ability to risk this somewhat superior health. He repeatedly chooses the unsafe course of action.

Threats to the therapist's mental health in the form of 'psychic infection' and 'countertransference psychosis' have already been discussed (see Chapter 4). Searles also mentions that, when his clients' fear that intimacy with the therapist will mean the latter's destruction, 'I do not attempt to be reassuring. . . . I have learned over and over again that these fears are not to be taken lightly' (1976b, p. 588). In deep transference involvements, Jung notes that the therapist serves as 'the last remaining shred of reality,' but that shred is sometimes a thread: 'Often the doctor is in much the same position as the alchemist who no longer knew whether he was melting the mysterious amalgam in the crucible or whether he was the salamander glowing in the fire' (1946, p. 199). Thus the therapist is sorely taxed, and willing to be.

As he repeatedly risks his better health over time, the analyst may gradually get more comfortable with the situation. He perhaps may find that the health/illness dichotomy begins to evaporate. This particular boundary at least becomes permeable, as is reflected in Jung's and Searles' overall viewpoint on psychopathology (see Chapter 3). This is not to say that risking one's health is ever easy. A sense of personal security in the therapist is not necessarily a given, as Searles' work so vividly indicates. It must always be re-discovered. Even if he could establish a position of safety, Jung for his part might encourage the therapist to abandon the theoretical preconceptions inherent in such a position (1937, 1950a). Nevertheless, it seems that the therapist will grow more fluid over time in both his internal and interpersonal health/illness boundaries. He may feel less threatened and more willing to contact the client, whose pathology gradually appears less 'pathological.'

As suggested above, the upshot of all this is that, just as health and illness become less dichotomized and more synthesized, so do therapist and client. The therapist becomes less an adversary and more a fellow of the client. In many ways they are on the same side, so to speak. The therapist, whose health after all is not that much greater and who has deep reserves of personal suffering, goes over to the client's world. It is a world in which the therapist has a personal and professional interest.

But another aspect of the therapist's mobility between worlds is that he is neither in one world nor the other. He – and the transference situation – is a bridge between the worlds of pathology and normality. At some point, in a successful treatment at least, the client will leave therapy. Yet the therapist always remains: by conscious choice he stays in perpetual contact with pathology, his own and his clients'. Sometimes in therapy it may even appear, to client and therapist alike, that the illness has been left to the doctor to struggle with when the client moves on (Searles, 1961g, 1968). But lest it seem that the therapist martyrs himself on the client's pathology, Searles interprets this situation as 'a transference in which the analyst personifies the patient's "older" – more accustomed – self which tends to feel left behind by, and jealous of, the new growth in the patient' (1971, p. 139). Thus it is not the final stage of treatment.

It is also evident that the patient's 'going' and the therapist's 'staying' are not clear-cut. The therapist does not exactly bridge the patient over to 'health,' but over to health as something like a 'health/illness' combination. As noted in Chapter 4, the goals of therapy do not consist of a care-free or introject-free future, but of a livable awareness of one's sore points. The therapist and the therapeutic process thus redefine mental health. This, too, is one of the roles of the therapist.

It has become clear that the therapist, originally fantasized to be a model of superior health, is also a model of illness, or better yet, a model of a 'health/illness' synthesis. He himself embodies the aims of psychotherapy: awareness, acceptance, access. The goals of therapy and the personality of the therapist, as described by Jung and Searles, are almost interchangeable. And what the client strives for is theoretically sitting right across from him.

Therefore the therapist models the future health of the client. But what kind of model is this? Clearly it is not a conscious model, nor a directive model. The therapist does not attempt to act out a good 'role' model, at least not in any particularized sense. He presents himself in his therapeutic identity, composed as it is of the many facets described above, none of which are so spectacular or even so desirable – but 'merely human' and hopefully therapeutic. For Jung and Searles, if the therapist needs to assume any role, it is this natural, 'human' role. And it is this role which the client unconsciously and gradually adopts. Jung describes the modeling activity in this way:

> Patients read the analyst's character intuitively, and they should find in him a man with failings, admittedly, but also a man who strives at every point to fulfill his human duties in the fullest sense.
>
> (Jung, 1914, p. 260)

The client identifies with the therapist's personality, and also with his unceasing effort. Furthermore, what the client sees the therapist struggling with is the *client's* personality, consisting particularly of complexes 'transferred' to and introjected by the therapist. Searles puts this most succinctly:

> The patient comes to see in the therapist all the figures of his own past, and these percepts have become now so free from anxiety that the patient can (partly by identification with the therapist who can accept within himself the reality nuclei for his being so perceived) discover them in himself, too . . . as really acceptable components of his own self.
>
> (Searles, 1976a, p. 532)

Thus the modeling comes not in the therapist's presentation of particularly outstanding qualities in his personality – of which, as described before, there may not be too many – but in the ongoing demonstration of his successful and failed attempts at awareness. This forms the basis for the unconscious patterning by the client. The therapist enacts daily what the client must learn to do in his life.

Does this mean that all clients must become therapists? Certainly not, though there are some metaphorical ways in which the client takes therapy with him when he goes (see Chapter 4). However, there are also some former clients, who decide not only to stay in therapy metaphorically but to become therapists themselves. The question is 'why?'

Searles and Jung strike different chords in their answers, though they are answers in accord with their respective theoretical presuppositions. Searles, in the course of describing parent–child attempts to literally 'drive each other crazy,' also shockingly suggests that therapists are prone to the same feelings toward their clients. As he graphically puts it, therapists have 'powerful, long-repressed desires to dismember the personality structure of other persons' (1959a, p. 278). The choice of profession is therefore a 'reaction-formation . . . against more than normally strong unconscious desires of this particular kind' – i.e., this aggressive, destructive kind (1959a, p. 278).

However, as Searles' general theoretical perspective changes over time, so does his view of the therapist's professional motivations. He says simply, 'We may have chosen this profession on the basis of unconscious guilt over having failed to cure our parents' (Searles, 1966a, p. 28). Still later, Searles expands this, conjecturing that future therapists, like future clients, act in childhood as *de facto* therapists to their apparently pathological families (1973a).[4] Their early lack of success in this endeavor is the source of the guilt they feel and the later compulsion to be a therapist. Clients seem to become the therapist's countertransference-parents.

In Searles' explanations it is striking how closely the therapist's motivations parallel patient motivations. The therapist is merely one step removed from the same dynamic forces that move clients. And he is 'one step removed' in two ways actually. First, his inclinations are directly channeled toward patients rather than parents, unconscious displacement notwithstanding. Second, these motivations should be more or less conscious to the therapist; the client by contrast is unconscious of his efforts to drive others crazy or cure them and is therefore only 'unconsciously a psychotherapist' (Searles, 1975a, p. 382).

Though explored in less detail and less reductively, Jung's versions of therapist motivations also come close to client motivations. Jung's outlook, in this context as in others, tends toward irrational, impersonal factors. His earliest statement suggests an innate 'special psychological gift' that at least encourages, if it does not motivate, the therapist toward his work (Jung, 1913, p. 200). Also evident is 'a serious concern with the molding of one's own character' (1913, p. 200). Thus an inherent ability to work psychologically with others, and a concern, really, with one's own self-realization, incline certain individuals to become therapists. Jung remains imprecise about the professional choice even in later writings. 'Presumably,' says Jung, the therapist 'had good reasons for choosing the profession of psychiatrist and for being particularly interested in the treatment of the psychoneuroses' (1946, p. 177). But Jung does not explain what the 'good reasons' are. He cites hidden, unconscious factors and downplays the element of 'free choice' (1946, p. 177).

But, as in his explanations of personality and pathology in general, the wellsprings in the unconscious seem to be archetypal. Jung can only suggest that inherited forces are at work, for he uses expressions like 'fateful disposition,' 'he did not choose his career by chance,' 'predestined' and 'instinctive disposition' (1946, p. 177). Jung never really specifies what archetypes might be operative here, though in later works he does express interest in 'the Greek myth of the wounded physician' (Jung, 1951b, p. 116) and in 'shamanism' (Jung, 1961a, p. 253). Both of these subject areas have to do with 'wounded' healers, who live eternally on the permeable border of disease and health.

The reasons for becoming a psychotherapist remain unclear, and Searles and Jung offer different explanations. They do agree on this, however: regardless of his deeper motivations, the analyst should have his own style. Many of this chapter's conclusions about the therapist's personality attributes are drawn from the descriptions Searles and Jung give of *themselves*. In addition, each man has developed his own theory and, as a consequence, his own sense of authority. They suggest, by example and directly, that the aspiring therapist should do likewise. Needless to say, if Jung and Searles did not think their own points of view valuable for others, they would not have published them. Yet a truly individual viewpoint is stressed by both, as indicated by Jung's comment, 'I can only hope and wish that no one becomes "Jungian" ' (1973b, p. 405). This idea, of course, is connected with Jung's larger idea of individuation, which fosters one's 'innermost, last and incomparable uniqueness . . . one's own self' (1928a, p. 173). Searles, while acknowledging that therapists can at times be 'almost paralyzedly concerned' with the opinions of colleagues, also emphasizes the importance of developing one's 'own particular, individual style' (1976b, pp. 600–1). He sums up his own and Jung's position nicely in a statement about psychotic patients that would seem applicable to almost all clients:

> Whatever one's individual abilities and limitations, it seems to me that only insofar as one can develop a mode of practice within which one can live and work with essential comfort and confidence, that one now has a strong base from which, and within which, to analyze the so-needful and so-demanding schizophrenic patient.
>
> (Searles, 1976b, p. 602)

Summary

There is an important area of Searles/Jung agreement: the therapist must use his personality as an instrument of therapy. As preparation for this, both theorists call for an extended analysis of the analyst, and an ongoing refinement and growth of his person through experience. The person who works on and through emotions also values affectivity in general. Only slight differences between Searles and Jung arise in these areas, consisting of Searles' more specific delineation of the therapist's post-analysis growth. Overall, personality as technique demands self-awareness, which is fostered in turn by the therapist's intuitive, nondefensive characteristics.

Both men's theories are congruent regarding the therapist's general expressiveness toward the client. A considered spontaneity is recommended and a totally neutral stance is criticized. The therapist also chooses honesty over solicitude in Searles' and Jung's view. The doctor's approach should be nondirective, with responsibility resting on the client.

In seeming contrast to the therapist's occasional bluntness, empathy is also championed by Jung and Searles. A capacity to experience love for the client is even mentioned. Both authors suggest that an unusual openness to others and to the unconscious enables these intimate contacts to happen. A further source of empathy is the therapist's own involvement with suffering and his tragic sense of life.

Searles and Jung equally admit that therapy can be a thankless profession. The choice to become a therapist is therefore an unconventional one. Though they differ on specifics, aspects of their theories also indicate that independent thinking and a critical intelligence are characteristic of the therapist.

Though there is inherent asymmetry in their positions, Jung and Searles agree on the therapist's equality with the patient. In and out of therapy, and in terms of intelligence, strength and growth, the therapist has much cause for humility. The therapist may find that he is the one who impedes progress. However, Searles and Jung each suggest that the therapist becomes increasingly willing to risk himself with clients and that client–therapist distinctions fade. The linkage to the client becomes still more evident when the theorists cite their close encounters with psychosis.

Finally, Jung and Searles coincide in placing the therapist perpetually on the border of illness. He shows the way out of illness to the client by modeling and redefining mental health. As to the therapist's choice of profession, Searles first notes sadistic and then guilt-oriented motivations, while Jung first mentions a personal, psychological inclination and then a fateful one. Though different, these opinions are consistent with other aspects of the writers' theories. They do agree, though, that a therapist must develop his own unique style.

6

CONCLUSIONS

The preceding chapters have shown that there are wide areas of agreement in the psychotherapies of Jung and Searles. Even when their theories diverge, it is only after some degree of congruence has been established. The acid test of congruence is whether apparent parallels hold up under closer scrutiny. In this study virtually every aspect of therapy that the authors themselves mention has been explored for overlap, and most reveal not only general but specific similarities.

Even at a general level the parallels between Searles and Jung are striking enough to be significant (e.g., the 'personified' unconscious, illness as potential health, analyst and patient both 'in therapy,' personality as technique, and so on). Paradoxically, dimensions of their viewpoints that seem disparate (e.g., the 'content' of interpretations, stages of therapy) prove to be more equivalent than not, while nominal parallels (e.g., 'self' and 'individuation') ultimately show contrast.

The similarities speak for themselves. However, although each apparent difference between Jung's and Searles' systems has been studied for latent similarities, there are certain kinds of differences that will not easily synthesize without violating them.

Probably their crucial difference – one that underlies many specific differences – is the contrast between Jung's 'collective' and Searles' 'personal' unconscious. This difference is, of course, a longstanding one between analytical psychology and psychoanalysis. The distinctive thing about Jung's theory is Jung's *addition* of the archetypal perspective, including issues of religious, synchronistic and transcendent dimensions. In effect, this addition furthers Searles' theory – but only if Jung's theory of the collective unconscious is accepted. From a perspective where both theories of the unconscious are valid, Jung's theory has personal *and* collective standpoints, whereas Searles has 'only' the personal.

Switching between the archetypal dimension and the personal – and to synthesize the two theories in this regard – involves a certain amount of dexterity. Indeed, it may take the kind of 'fluidity' that Searles describes regarding his own sense of personal identity (1966–7, p. 68). An archetypal viewpoint means a teleological, symbolic approach as opposed to a more analytic, historical one. It places The Unconscious in a much grander light than the personal 'unconscious' (as in the different terms 'Self' and 'self'). Jung tends more to trust the power of, or entrust power in, the unconscious as a supraordinate force. Searles, and psychoanalysis, tends to have a respectful but less religious attitude toward the unconscious. The two attitudes need not be mutually exclusive. Intellectually, their synthesis rests on the assumption that the two perspectives, personal and archetypal, are two versions or two possible explanations of the same reality.

A closely related fundamental difference between Searles and Jung pertains to the *focus* of many of their descriptions. Jungian theory by and large stays close to the unconscious point of view, while Searles tends toward the attitude of consciousness. Jung gives the unconscious a voice of its own and presents the unconscious more in its own language. In contrast, Searles essentially uses the categories and contents of consciousness to delineate the unconscious. His view also has a certain internal logic that Jung's, which again is oriented toward a more magical realm of the unconscious, does not have.

For instance, Searles' belief that personality and pathology are formed out of introjections and projections within the family (and then transferentially re-worked via the analyst–patient relationship) appeals to the conscious mind. It is an orderly dynamic, however invisible its mechanisms. On the other hand, Jung's historical, ancestral or 'fateful' constructs speak directly to the intuitive, transcendent and 'synchronistic' qualities of the unconscious itself (Jung, 1952a, p. 437). Searles basically doubts that there is anything transcendent in the unconscious, subjective experience of individuals (1960). He goes about as far with the rationalistic view of psychotherapy as one can go, then Jung takes over. It is not clear who furthers whom here – it depends on one's point of view on transcendence. Nevertheless, their different foci can be effectively complementary.

From another vantage point, it is also true that Searles' rationalistic explanation and focus on the personal unconscious enable his theory to further Jung's in precisely these regards. Jung is somewhat thin on the personal unconscious and its relation to psychotherapy, relative to his wealth of material on the archetypal. It is evident that, after his departure from psycho-analysis proper, Jung chose (or was forced) to rush headlong into his description of the collective unconscious. This enormous task included in-depth excursions into mythology, fairy tales, alchemy and the religions of the world. Jung's range is enormous and his knowledge encyclopedic, but it leaves his description of the personal unconscious back on the shore, so to speak.

Of course that is the way Jung saw it and wanted it. But his investment in the collective unconscious also highlights another fundamental divergence from Searles. Except in terms of personality theory and dream interpretation, Searles is con-sistently more detailed and precise than Jung. As this study shows, the authors frequently say the same thing or point in the same direction. But Searles fills in more of the specifics and provides extensive, ongoing examples. In the vital areas of analytic technique and transference, Searles offers more that the practicing therapist can hold on to.

Part of the way Searles furthers Jung in this respect is related to the previously mentioned difference that Jung is a spokesman more for the unconscious and Searles for the conscious mind. Searles also is very much a spokesman for the *therapist*. One of his major contributions is the depth and openness with which he explores the therapist's reactions and overall perspective during the therapy process. Jung retains his emphasis on the unconscious and its symbolism at almost all times. His intensive study of transference (Jung, 1946) and even his detailed individual case studies (Jung, 1928–30, 1944, 1950a, 1976) focus almost entirely on the general movements of the unconscious rather than the continuous, therapist–client interaction.

In this respect, then, Searles furthers Jung, though it might be said that Jung's descriptions of the 'unconscious' sharply outline the patient's point of view. Together, Jung's 'client' view and Searles' 'therapist' view form a useful, integrated whole. Jung's intent, however, is less to illuminate the client or therapist than to elucidate the collective unconscious. His ideas can speak to a general, non-clinical audience, whereas Searles' writings really

147

cannot. Probably neither Searles nor Jung ultimately has more to offer the clinician, however; they merely offer it in different ways: Searles by speaking directly to the therapist about 'countertransference' and technique, Jung by speaking indirectly to the clinician about the nature of the unconscious. Stated differently, Jung describes the unconscious 'as it is,' whereas Searles frequently centers on the unconscious as it is in the therapist.

A corollary to the fact that Searles speaks to the therapist and Jung to the general audience, is that Searles' system is more clinically applicable in the majority of cases than Jung's. Jung's orientation and content cause him to be either overlooked or inaccessible to many therapists. In fact, Jung's is really a two-tiered model of psychotherapy consisting of: 1) psychotherapy as it is usually known and 2) the individuation process. His attention turns increasingly to the latter of these two aspects of analysis over the years (see Chapter 1). 'Individuation' (in the Jungian, second-half-of-life or 'numinous' sense) is not within the theoretical or experiential realms of most therapists. Hence the numinous, and Jung, are not in their therapeutic modalities either. Therefore Searles, who shows much technical similarity with Jung, can further him by bringing him back toward the 'psychotherapy' mainstream. Searles' techniques help ground Jung's theories of the collective unconscious.

By the same token, though, Searles is extended through Jung's explorations of human purpose and 'meaning.' The cognitive aspect of cure is crucial in both men's theories, as is the notion that human suffering is not fundamentally alleviated but adapted to. It would seem that the latter can finally be achieved only through the development of some kind of organized, philosophical framework. Searles' theory implicitly suggests a deep, psycho-dynamic, rational model of human existence. The body of his work also provides a set of fairly benevolent views of life. Love, for example, runs deeper than hatred (Searles, 1958b, 1965b) or a patient or child may almost literally sacrifice his life as a 'symbiotic therapist' to his crippled parents (1973a, p. 174). But Searles does not spend much time on the broader implications of all this. However, some people (and some clients) seem to need more than this. 'Meaning' in the wider, more metaphysical sense is something Jung's theory provides better access to. Much as Jung suggests that the archetype is instinct 'raised to a higher

148

frequency'(1954a, p. 212), so his archetypal perspective in general can pitch Searles' analytic-reductive approach to a more meaningful level.

Viewed together and from a distance, it would at first appear that Searles has most to offer to a theory of psychotherapy and Jung to a philosophy of life. Therefore a whole is provided by integrating the two. Ironically, one way this synthesis manifests itself is in a difference that runs through all the chapters of this study. Repeatedly, the explanation for areas of divergence in their theories is that their clients are vastly different. Though the question is raised in Chapter 3 whether their respective clienteles do not in fact overlap diagnostically, Searles' major attention is centered on very schizophrenic patients. Jung's clients, in contrast, seem to be advanced, normal-neurotic people (at least the ones he writes about are). They can function in the world, whereas many of Searles' are hospitalized.

This distinction gives rise to a number of points, previously mentioned and otherwise. It partly explains, for instance, why Searles appears more 'clinical,' more applicable and more concerned with psychotherapy. It explains why Jung is and can be more concerned with 'meaning' in the therapeutic process, and why he is considered grandiose or mystical by therapists who have neither 'numinous' experiences nor 'numinous' clients. The type of patients each man has explains Searles' concern with basic ego-formation and Jung's with highly esoteric ego-transformation, as well as their different versions of individuation.

Since Searles works with the more common, more disturbed type of client, it is tempting to infer, as above, that his psychotherapy theory is more applicable to all clients than Jung's is. To the pragmatist, Jungian analysis may seem like a luxury for the chosen few, a course in advanced personality growth.

However, the idea of Searles for the 'people' and Jung for the 'elite' is a deceptive one. First of all, both theorists claim a universality for their theories (see Chapter 2) and, second, Jung is also deeply rooted in work with schizophrenics. After all it was Jung's 'Psychology of Dementia Praecox' (1907) that brought Freudian psychology into the psychiatric domain, and Searles who insists, against increasingly 'pharmacological' trends, that it still belongs there (1976b, p. 591). More important, though, is the fact that, if Jung's range of clients seems narrow, then *so is Searles'*.

149

Over a fourteen-year span from 1951 to 1965, Searles reportedly psychoanalyzed a total of only eighteen psychotic patients (Knight, 1965). His normal hospital caseload was six clients (Searles, 1980). Add to this his private practice caseload and it is probable that Searles' breadth of experience, client-wise, is no wider than Jung's. Apparently both theorists focus their writing on the *ends* of the client spectrum: Jung at the more 'intact' end and Searles at the opposite, unformed end. Overall, it may be that both Jung and Searles have a restricted range, limited to the extremes and leaving out the middle. In strictly quantitative, cost/benefit terms, Searles' long-term analyses – four or five sessions per week for a decade or more with chronic schizophrenics – are no more 'practical' than Jung's work with 'individuating' clients.

But here avenues of synthesis on this 'client' issue begin to arise. It becomes apparent that Searles and Jung meet not in the quantitative but in the qualitative, 'depth' dimension of their theories. Less interested in a democratic approach to therapy for all clients, their writings push forward into new territory for some clients and for understanding man in general. From different directions, they go deep rather than wide. In a sense both Searles and Jung are as much researchers as clinicians. Jung even suggests, implicitly and inadvertently, that individuation may be only for analysts: 'The recognition of anima and animus is a specific experience that seems to be reserved mostly, or at any rate primarily, for psychotherapists' (1951a, p. 267). Searles' attentions, too, are directed mainly toward the therapist, albeit in a different way than Jung's. Both theorists' researches clearly have much to offer the therapist, personally and professionally.

Perhaps neither man's theories are applicable to the majority of psychotherapy clients. But that is not the question. Both authors claim universality for their findings and, most importantly for this study, their differences in clientele can be brought to a synthesis. Though derived, perhaps, from clients on opposing ends of the diagnostic scale, Jung's 'advanced growth' perspective combined with Searles' 'basic growth' perspective form one, complete perspective. The fact, indicated throughout this study, that their descriptions of psychotherapy are quite similar allows this synthesis. That is, both types of clients they serve apparently demand more or less the same methods of therapy. Searles and Jung use the same means to different ends.

CONCLUSIONS

Though synthesizable in the same manner as the 'client' difference above, and perhaps related to it, another difference in evidence throughout this study is the intrapsychic (Jung) vs. the interpersonal (Searles). On theoretical levels, Jung and Searles correspond almost completely in their belief that the external world is the carrier of a more crucial, subjective dimension. Therefore, outer entanglements of all kinds, especially relationships, suggest inner complications. While both theorists begin with this 'inner,' intrapsychic assumption, they then go consistently in opposite directions with it. In a sense Jung goes farther 'in' with it, toward the objective psyche or collective unconscious. Meanwhile Searles goes farther 'out' – back out, in effect, into the external world. Above all both men tend to *work* with the intrapsychic differently: hence Searles' greater detail on the 'reality' in projection and on therapist–client interaction, and Jung's greater precision on interpretation and the 'symbolic' way. Because Searles and Jung have the same theoretical base, however, their two therapy directions can be seen as complementary rather than irreconcilably different. They tend to balance rather than alienate each other.

This potential synthesis of the intrapsychic and interpersonal means that the practicing therapist may use either emphasis as a matter of technique. This depends, of course, on a number of factors, including the particular client, the therapist's personal inclination, the stage of therapy perhaps, or failure or impasse with one of the techniques. Either way, the effect should be more or less the same, because of the common, 'unconscious' dynamics of change.

A corollary to the intra-/inter- difference and synthesis is to approach the authors via typology. Given his interest in the intra-psychic, the symbolic, the 'unconscious' *per se* and 'theory,' Jung seems to fall into the thinking and intuition realm. His focus is a little 'outside' of this world, indeed, often in the fantasy world. In contrast, Searles is 'here' and writes about the interpersonal, 'psychotherapy,' the therapy session itself and the 'feelings' between people. Hence, one way to view their theoretical differences and to synthesize them is to characterize the theorists themselves, in Jungian terms, as 'thinking–intuitive' (Jung) vs. 'feeling–sensation' (Searles). Oversimplified though this may be, it accounts for differences without polarizing them.

Another way to synthesize their theories is touched on in most

151

chapters. The question of which of their views is 'correct' arises implicitly every time differences are mentioned. Is psychopathology an irrupting archetype or a damaged introject? Is the unconscious 'personal' or 'collective'? Is talking of one's personal past a fantasy way of talking about archetypes or is talking about archetypes a defense against the personal? One can answer these questions according to a subjective, epistemological or 'majority' preference. However, one may also choose to see Jung and Searles as two versions of or two languages for a fundamental 'unconscious' reality. Just as psychotherapies are about equally effective and therefore potentially synthesizable (Smith *et al.*, 1981), so Jung and Searles may simply be speaking in different terms about the same things happening in the unconscious. This is not to say that all theories are valid, but that, given their vast overlap, Searles and Jung are closer to each other than to others. It may also mean that it does not matter what one works on in therapy, but it is important to work on something. And the best place to start is with the personally meaningful, in whatever form it presents itself. If Jung's is a therapy for people who want 'gods' in their lives and if Searles' is for those who prefer less 'mystical' concepts, so be it. 'Humanistic' (Jung) or merely 'humane' (Searles): both models will touch the unconscious.

These then are some general differences, some suggestions of superiority in one theory or the other, and some ways of synthesis. Significant parallels at specific or general levels are *ipso facto* or already synthesized. They really need no further explanation. With this detailed, top-to-bottom and from-all-sides inspection of Jung and Searles thus having produced certain areas of synthesis, some implications of their now collective view of psychotherapy and some general observations about their theories, separately and together, are in order.

A key element in Searles' and Jung's therapies is actually the absence of an element; namely the absence of any stated concern with behavior change as such. It is not so much that the theorists do not want clients to change their lives in outward, tangible ways – obviously they want clients to live life more fully – it is simply that Jung and Searles almost never define personality change as behavior change. Behavioristic concerns are widespread in psychotherapy today, even in the most 'psychological,' non-materialistic models. Personality is 'action,' what one 'does' is what one 'is.' Searles and Jung, however, prefer to interpret

152

actions as reflections of the personality rather than *the* personality. Behavior is one step removed from one's 'self,' unless interpreted back toward the self. And behavior change is a secondary phenomenon in their theories, not because of a selective bias in this study but because Jung and Searles focus on what they consider to be a more fundamental, interior level.

This type of theoretical emphasis explains not only their particular definitions of pathology and health, but a deeper belief that the insane are not necessarily so 'insane.' The behavior of the insane certainly *looks* crazy, though it may be true that 'abnormal' people must bear the brunt of 'normal' people's fearful projections of their own impulsivity, aggression, bizarreness or even individuality. By attending to personality rather than behavior, Searles and Jung short-circuit these attributions. Along these same lines, their therapies attempt to treat the whole (or 'not yet' whole) personality rather than the pathology apparently shown in the behavior.

The issue of projection, noted above, receives regal treatment in both men's writings and work. It is evident that people, including analysts, can tolerate in others only what they can imagine and tolerate in themselves. This simple statement turns out to be super-charged for Jung and Searles, forming the cornerstone of their ideas about personality, pathology, therapy and the therapist's role. In addition to being an act of 'identity' or 'identification,' projection is moreover an act of omnipotence or narcissism – an assumption that the world is as one imagines it. The questioning of this assumption is very important to both theorists, and it is unusually 'new' and perhaps even earth-shaking for a client to grasp it and its implications. Its importance is such that both authors develop very highly sophisticated views of projection, beyond the simple suggestion (but difficult reality) of 'withdrawing' projections. The precise mechanism of projection–integration they espouse seems to follow the sequence of projection as: 1) it is 'you,' 2) it is 'not you' and therefore 'me,' 3) it is 'partly you' and 'partly me' (hooks, reality nuclei), but 'I' will take responsibility for it in me. Therefore, working with the projection concept entails a complex, fundamental process of separation and individuation.

Clinically speaking, the most important kind of projections are those that take place in analysis – the transference. The importance Jung and Searles place on the projection issue transfers, so to speak, to therapy itself. Transference is the crux of therapy in their systems and they go a long way toward redefining it. Traditionally, transference is thought of as the client's projections of his parental complexes or introjects onto the therapist. Jung and Searles stress its unconscious and countertransference aspects, respectively, and they stress them in essentially health-giving, purposeful ways. The result is a definition of the transference phenomenon in its entirety as, simply but meaningfully: the unconscious relationship between the client and the therapist, *both* ways.

The subtlety and difficulty of this relationship burdens the participants and, in a manner of speaking, burdens psychotherapy as a whole. It becomes clear for both theorists that real therapy often begins at those moments when the participants are lost or confused (*ambivalent symbiosis, nigredo*) or close to an almost total experience of the unconscious (*full symbiosis, coniunctio*). That is, the dynamics of cure begin when neither client nor therapist fully understands what is happening – at moments of impasse. Evidently one must be lost in order to be found.

With the 'true' therapy beginning to actualize, ironically, at the moment when therapy looks blocked, insuring continuity becomes a necessity. Not just the therapist himself but the psychotherapy process overall must become a 'protected circle.' Therapy not only nurtures a 'self' for the client, it symbolizes that self in its sustained, resilient solidity. The process, when it works, endures and survives all things, even the deadlocks it seems to demand. In this sense, or perhaps from the point of view of the unconscious, 'psychotherapy' is the self, a sort of 'process' mandala.

Psychotherapy is sometimes thought of as an educative or 'learning' process. For Searles and Jung, however, this is probably not an apt metaphor. Since, as above, therapy creates and represents the self simultaneously, and since it holds both participants in its relentless 'grip,' it is not an education process of the usual sort. As defined by Jung and Searles, the learning is experiential and creative, with cognitive growth following out of but never ahead of feeling changes. Hence the attitude of the participants is receptive and slowly waiting rather than actively acquisitive of knowledge. Unlike teacher and student, the partners are ultimately equal in stature and often equally ignorant of what is to be learned. Often, too, the client is the teacher, while the therapist must study and understand the material and the person being presented. Thus, for both Searles and Jung, therapy means mutual discovery and intense personal involvement. This is 'education' in the best sense of the word.

From all this, and from the particulars of such therapy aspects as 'phylogenetic regression' and 'pathology as potential,' it becomes clear that Jung and Searles assume there is a fundamental human drive toward health, growth and meaning. Their basic view of the human condition, while cautious, is hopeful. A sort of unconscious 'health-vector' underlies their approach and attitude to therapy and encourages them to trust the treatment process. Resting on this sense of confidence, their theories frequently ennoble man. This positive outlook, for instance, is at work when Searles points out the heroic, symbiotic sacrifice of the child on behalf of his parents, or when Jung stresses man's thirst for spiritual meaning. Whether accurate or not, these theories elevate human potential.

A related development is that Jung and Searles stand revealed as something like 'honesty' therapists. In the final analysis they would seem to believe that the truth, though it may make one miserable, *will* make one free. Integrity is effective, and the means to the ends of therapy (or anything else) must be correct or else the goal is not truly achieved. Therefore they trust most of all to experience 'as it is,' and report their findings at some risk to their personal reputation. Searles is stunning in his personal candor and public revelations, and Jung is unguarded in his attempts to incorporate the 'irrational' into scientific discussion.

An historical continuity, a sense of context, is important in all things. Searles is the next generation after Jung, and together they span twentieth-century psychoanalysis – in time if not in traditionalism. There is a continuity of thought, too, within their respective theories. Each man discusses and considers the same issues over time, refining and deepening basic concepts. Thus, from his early works on occult phenomena and complex theory (1902, 1907), Jung weaves his way into more encompassing, archetypal thought (1928a, 1936a). Or, for Searles, the client's need to affect the therapist personally (1949/79), later shows up in the client's becoming 'indispensably important' to the therapist (1973a, p. 190). Similarly, Searles' earlier sense of 'outrage' (1961g, p. 544) at the client's illness ripens into the later sarcasm, 'It couldn't be happening to a nicer guy' (1976a, p. 516). Perhaps any creative thinker has only a few 'great' ideas, which he then

155

proceeds to elucidate over the years. From a retrospective viewpoint, one can see fundamental concepts develop, deepen and thread their way through Searles' and Jung's work.

It is evident, too, that writing serves a special purpose for both theorists, something more than sharing information with colleagues or the public. Writing is a way of assimilating and understanding their clients and themselves, a way of enriching experience and making it as conscious as possible – a process like therapy itself.

Closing thoughts

The primary contribution of this study consists in its comparison and integration of Jung and Searles, which has not been done before in a detailed, systematic fashion. The specifics of a psychotherapy model based on their theories are here. But this book makes a number of other contributions and points toward issues for further research.

For students of Searles, this study provides a summary of his psychotherapy model. It is the first synopsis by someone other than Searles himself, and the first of any kind to discuss his work at length across standard psychotherapy dimensions. Similarly, though Jung (1935a, 1951a, 1961a) makes some tentative moves in this direction, a detailed and complete summary of his psychotherapy as such has not been presented in an organized form that speaks directly to the therapist.

To analytical psychology (Jungian psychology) the value of the theories of Harold Searles has been demonstrated in depth here for the first time. And particularly for those Jungians who already have passing or deeper acquaintance with Searles' model, this thesis suggests lines of exploration. Jungian psychology clearly has something to gain from Searles. In order to be more widely applicable, Jung's theory needs bolstering around issues of basic, ego growth. Jungian clinical theory has been in sore need of elucidation. Searles provides this in a fashion most congruent with fundamental tenets of Jungian thought. He helps bring Jung back to the clinic, and back to the mainstream of psychotherapy.

By the same token, this book suggests how Jungian approaches can further psychoanalysis itself, at least for the branch of contemporary psychoanalysis in which Searles fits. Less constrained by the polemical considerations of early years, modern psychoanalysis can explore taboo areas and taboo analysts, both within its ranks (Searles) and outside them (Jung). Particularly in the analysis of the schizophrenic client, Jung, who has proved so similar to Searles in this book, has much to offer in terms of theory and practice. In his work and personal experience Jung has ventured deep into the unconscious and, like Searles, has returned and articulated something of great importance for the practitioner.

In terms of psychotherapy research, comparing and linking Searles and Jung has produced an intriguing version of the common, 'nonspecific' factors involved in healing. Since just about all therapies work (Smith *et al.*, 1981), the question of why or what *in general* works is paramount. Jung and Searles suggest a model with roots in the Freudian past (transference) and even as far back as shamanism. Psychotherapy works by means of personality and 'corrective' personal relationships rather than techniques – these are not entirely new concepts. But the ideas of a deep, even two-way, exchange of 'health' and 'illness' and of a profound, mutual transformation of personalities are dynamic and radical. Cure comes through the unconscious, through dimensions of perpetual illness in the therapist and therapeutic strivings in the client. If not at work in all therapies, these factors are certainly worthy of consideration.

For research attempting synthesis of theories, the process undertaken in this study suggests that, paradoxically, outlining differences with precision can lead toward integration. Differences can provide complementary material if the researcher has a non-preferential, non-competitive approach – no axe to grind. It is important, however, that there be some initial points of overlap on at least a general level. This gives synthesis some roots to grow from and prevents a violent splitting apart at moments of divergence.

Finally, for any person integrating disparate viewpoints, the process embodied in this study is important. A thorough, up-and-down study, over time and across categories, permits understanding to grow organically, in heart as well as mind. Synthesis must be experienced to be real. Likewise, the learner must know that no theory of psychotherapy will tell him what to do and how to be, and that the only way to *know* a theory is to interpret and explore one's personal psychology through it. Some of this is reflected in these closing comments by Jung and Searles respectively:

I am astonished, disappointed, pleased with myself. I am distressed, depressed, rapturous. I am all these things at once, and cannot add up the sum. . . . There is nothing I am quite sure about. . . . I exist on the foundation of something I do not know.

(Jung, 1961b, p. 358)

Somewhere midway through my own analysis, after I had undergone much change, I visualized the core of myself as being, nonetheless, like a steel ball bearing, with varicolored sectors on its surface. At least, I told myself, this would not change. I have long since lost any such image of the core of my identity; it became dissolved in grief, and my sense of identity now possesses something of the fluidity of tears.

(Searles, 1966–7, p. 68)

NOTES

1 INTRODUCTION

1 See Jacoby (1981, 1984, 1990), Schwartz-Salant (1982) and Satinover (1984).
2 See Goodheart (1980, 1984) and Parks (1987).
3 See Young-Eisendrath (1984) and Sullivan (1987, 1989).
4 See, for example, Kugler and Hillman (1985) and Samuels (1985).
5 This is readily apparent in Langs and Searles (1980), a book from which Goodheart draws much of his review.
6 All this is not to condemn Goodheart's work (and Langs'), which is extremely important, but to note that the work on a Jung/Searles synthesis has yet to be done.
7 See *Symbols of Transformation* (1911–12/1952), *The Visions Seminars* (1930–4), 'A Study in the Process of Individuation' (1934e), 'Individual Dream Symbolism in Relation to Alchemy' (1936c) as examples.
8 Perhaps the best overview of this pioneering work (and of current Jungian practice in general) is Andrew Samuels' *Jung and the Post-Jungians* (1985), a book which is, among other things, a response to the 'groundswell' of modern clinical interest in Jung. The book is also a monumental synthetic effort in itself.
9 Michael Fordham's *Jungian Psychotherapy* (1978), while implicitly coordinating Freudian and Kleinian perspectives with Jung's, does not have this as its primary goal.
10 Including Jungian contexts (cf. Fordham, 1969, 1979; Goodheart, 1980; Schwartz-Salant, 1982; Ulanov, 1982; Samuels, 1985; Young-Eisendrath and Weidemann, 1987; Sullivan, 1989).
11 Recent books on countertransference seem to underestimate by near omission Searles' original contributions (see Tansey and Burke, 1987; Gorkin, 1989).
12 See Winnicott (1964), Ellenberger (1970), Atwood and Stolorow (1977) and, for a Jungian perspective, Fordham (1975, 1978) and Satinover (1984, 1985).

159

2 THEORETICAL CONSIDERATIONS

1 This has important implications for psychotherapy.

3 PSYCHOPATHOLOGY

1 As R.D. Laing says, 'What is meant precisely by good, bad and mad we do not yet know' (1965, p. 181).
2 See Atwood and Stolorow (1977), who state this rather directly.
3 Note, however, Searles' further comments that such experiences may be linked with 'turning points,' 'restitution' following emotional disasters, and 'recovery-through-phylogenetic-regression' (1960, p. 107). This is quite close to Jung's compensatory notions concerning the Self and the constellation of Self-symbols.
4 See Schwartz-Salant (1986, 1988a, 1988b) for a neo-Jungian understanding of this idea.
5 Kohut's (1971, 1977) concepts seem quite relevant here, though it is unclear if he was acquainted with Searles' work in this area (Searles, 1984, p. 380).

4 THE PROCESS OF PSYCHOTHERAPY

1 This conception has linkages with psychoanalytic conceptions of the 'therapeutic' or 'working alliance' (Zetzel, 1956; Greenson, 1967) and neo-Jungian ideas around the 'patient-healer' archetype (Guggenbuhl-Craig, 1971; Groesbeck, 1975).
2 'Transference' will be used in this book as shorthand for the more accurate term 'transference/countertransference.'
3 Searles appears to make much greater use of the couch in his out-patient work with patients who are less disturbed, usually, than his Chestnut Lodge clientele.
4 This term may have its origins in mesmerism (see Carotenuto, 1991), though its use here may be an artifact of translation of Jung's works into English.
5 See Langs and Searles (1980) for an interesting discussion of this facet of Langs' theories.

5 THE THERAPIST

1 For discussion, and some criticism by a Jungian, of Jung's 'less organized behavior,' see Fordham (1978).
2 Winnicott (1968) raises important questions about the patient's achievement of the capacity to 'use' the analyst.
3 This appears to be closely related to the narcissistic transferences of which Heinz Kohut (1971, 1977) later spoke. See also Plaut (1956) on 'incarnating the archetype' for a Jungian perspective.
4 This line of Searles' thinking has been picked up by recent therapies

concerned with 'dysfunctional' families, adult children of alcoholics, gifted children meeting parents' narcissistic needs, and so on.

BIBLIOGRAPHY

Arlow, J. (1979) 'Psychoanalysis', in R. Corsini (ed.) *Current Psychotherapies*, 3rd edn, Itasca: Peacock Publishers.

Atwood, G. and Stolorow, R. (1977) 'Metapsychology, Reification and the Representational World of C.G. Jung', *International Review of Psychoanalysis*, 4: 197–214.

Bateson, G., Jackson, D., Haley, J. and Weakland, J. (1956) 'Toward a Theory of Schizophrenia', *Behavioral Science*, 1: 251.

Brome, V. (1978) *Jung*, New York: Atheneum.

Brown, J.A.C. (1961) *Freud and the Post-Freudians*, Harmondsworth: Penguin Books.

Carotenuto, A. (1982) *A Secret Symmetry: Sabina Spielrein Between Jung and Freud*, New York: Pantheon Books.

—— (1991) *Kant's Dove: The History of Transference in Psychoanalysis*, Willmette: Chiron.

Cohen, M.B. (1952) 'Countertransference and Anxiety', *Psychiatry*, 15: 231–43.

Coles, R. (1975) *The Mind's Fate*, Boston: Little, Brown.

Ehrenwald, J. (1976) *The History of Psychotherapy*, New York: Aronson.

Ellenberger, H. (1970) *The Discovery of the Unconscious*, New York: Basic Books.

Ellis, A. (1979) 'Rational-Emotive Therapy', in R. Corsini (ed.) *Current Psychotherapies*, 3rd edn, Itasca: Peacock Publishers.

Evans, R. (1976) *R.D. Laing: The Man and His Ideas*, New York: Dutton.

Fordham, M. (1962) 'An Evaluation of Jung's Work', Lecture #119, presented to the Guild of Pastoral Psychology, London, 1962.

—— (1969) 'Technique and Countertransference', in M. Fordham, R. Gordon, J. Hubback and K. Lambert (eds) *Technique in Jungian Analysis*, London: Heinemann, 1974.

—— (1975) 'Memories and Thoughts about C.G. Jung', *Journal of Analytical Psychology*, 20: 107–13.

—— (1978) *Jungian Psychotherapy*, New York: Wiley.

—— (1979) 'Analytical Psychology and Countertransference', *Contemporary Psychoanalysis*, 15: 630–46.

Freeman, J. (1959) 'The "Face to Face" Interview', in W. Maguire and R.F.C.

Hull (eds) *C.G. Jung Speaking*, Princeton: Princeton University Press, 1977.

Freud, S. (1909) 'Notes Upon a Case of Obsessional Neurosis', *The Standard Edition of the Complete Psychological Works of Sigmund Freud*, Vol. 10, London: Hogarth.

—— (1910) 'The Future Prospects of Psychoanalytic Therapy', *Therapy and Technique*, New York: Collier, 1963.

—— (1912) 'Recommendations for Physicians on the Psychoanalytic Method of Treatment', *Therapy and Technique*, New York: Collier, 1963.

—— (1913) 'Further Recommendations in the Technique of Psychoanalysis: On Beginning the Treatment. The Question of the First Communications. The Dynamics of the Cure', *Therapy and Technique*, New York: Collier, 1963.

—— (1914) 'On the History of the Psychoanalytic Movement', *Therapy and Technique*, New York: Collier, 1963.

Frey-Rohn, L. (1976) *From Freud to Jung*, New York: Delta.

Friedman, P. and Goldstein, J. (1964) 'Some Comments on the Psychology of C.G. Jung', *Psychoanalytic Quarterly*, 33: 194–225.

Fromm, E. (1963) 'C.G. Jung: Prophet of the Unconscious', *Scientific American*, 209: 283–90.

Gendlin, E. (1979) 'Experiential Psychotherapy', in R. Corsini (ed.) *Current Psychotherapies*, 3rd edn, Itasca: Peacock Publishers.

Glover, E. (1956) *Freud or Jung?*, New York: Meridian Books.

Goodheart, W. (1980) 'A Theory of Analytic Interaction', *Library Journal of the C.G. Jung Institute of San Francisco*, 1: 1–39.

—— (1984) 'Successful and Unsuccessful Interventions in Jungian Analysis: The Construction and Destruction of the Spellbinding Circle', *Chiron*, 1984: 89–117.

Gorkin, M. (1989) *The Uses of Countertransference*, New York: Aronson.

Greenson, R. (1967) *The Technique and Practice of Psychoanalysis*, Vol. 1, New York: International Universities Press.

Groesbeck, C.J. (1975) 'The Archetypal Image of the Wounded Healer', *Journal of Analytical Psychology*, 20: 122–45.

Guggenbuhl-Craig, A. (1971) *Power in the Helping Professions*, Zurich: Spring.

Guntrip, H. (1961) *Personality and Human Interaction*, New York: International Universities Press.

Gurman, A. and Kniskern, D. (eds) (1981) *Handbook of Family Therapy*, New York: Brunner/Mazel.

Hall, C. and Lindszay, G. (1978) *Theories of Personality*, 3rd edn, New York: Wiley.

Hannah, B. (1976) *Jung: His Life and Work*, New York: Putnam's.

Harms, E. (1962) 'C.G. Jung', *American Journal of Psychiatry*, 118: 728–32.

Heimann, P. (1950) 'On Counter-transference', *International Journal of Psychoanalysis*, 31: 81–4.

Henderson, J. (1975) 'C.G. Jung: A Reminiscent Picture of his Method', *Journal of Analytical Psychology*, 20: 114–21.

Jacobi, J. (1965) *The Way of Individuation*, New York: Harcourt, Brace and World.

Jacoby, M. (1981) 'Reflections on Heinz Kohut's Concept of Narcissism', *Journal of Analytical Psychology*, 26: 19–32.

—— (1984) *The Analytic Encounter: Transference and Human Relationship*, Toronto: Inner City Books.

—— (1990) *Individuation and Narcissism: The Psychology of Self in Jung and Kohut*, London: Routledge.

Jung, C.G. *The Collected Works of C.G. Jung*, 20 vols, H. Read, M. Fordham, G. Adler and W. McGuire (eds), trans. R.F.C. Hull (except vol. 2, trans. Leopold Stein), Bollingen Series XX, Princeton: Princeton University Press. [Hereafter this collection will be referred to as *Collected Works*.]

—— (1902) 'On the Psychology and Pathology of So-called Occult Phenomena', *Collected Works*, Volume 1.

—— (1905) 'On the Psychological Diagnosis of Evidence', *Collected Works*, Volume 2.

—— (1907) 'The Psychology of Dementia Praecox', *Collected Works*, Volume 3.

—— (1909) 'The Significance of the Father in the Destiny of the Individual', *Collected Works*, Volume 4.

—— (1911) 'On the Doctrine of Complexes', *Collected Works*, Volume 2.

—— (1911–12/1952) *Symbols of Transformation*, *Collected Works*, Volume 5.

—— (1912) 'New Paths in Psychology', *Collected Works*, Volume 7.

—— (1913) 'The Theory of Psychoanalysis', *Collected Works*, Volume 4.

—— (1914) 'Some Crucial Points in Psychoanalysis: A Correspondence between Dr Jung and Dr Loy', *Collected Works*, Volume 4.

—— (1916a) 'The Transcendent Function', *Collected Works*, Volume 8.

—— (1916b) 'Adaptation, Individuation, Collectivity', *Collected Works*, Volume 18.

—— (1917) 'On the Psychology of the Unconscious', *Collected Works*, Volume 7.

—— (1919) 'Instinct and the Unconscious', *Collected Works*, Volume 8.

—— (1920) 'The Psychological Foundations of Belief in Spirits', *Collected Works*, Volume 8.

—— (1921) *Psychological Types*, *Collected Works*, Volume 6.

—— (1926) 'Analytical Psychology and Education', *Collected Works*, Volume 17.

—— (1928a) 'The Relations between the Ego and the Unconscious', *Collected Works*, Volume 7.

—— (1928b) 'On Psychic Energy', *Collected Works*, Volume 8.

—— (1928c) 'The Therapeutic Value of Abreaction', *Collected Works*, Volume 16.

—— (1928d) 'Child Development and Education', *Collected Works*, Volume 17.

—— (1928–30) 'Dream Analysis', 4th edn, unpublished seminar notes compiled by the C.G. Jung Institute, Zurich.

—— '(1929a) 'Freud and Jung: Contrasts', *Collected Works*, Volume 4.

—— (1929b) 'Commentary', *The Secret of the Golden Flower*, trans. Richard Wilhelm, New York: Harcourt, Brace and World.

—— (1929c) 'Problems of Modern Psychotherapy', *Collected Works*, Volume 16.

—— (1930–4) *The Visions Seminars*, New York: Spring.

—— (1931a) 'A Psychological Theory of Types', *Collected Works*, Volume 6.

—— (1931b) 'The Structure of the Psyche', *Collected Works*, Volume 8.

—— (1931c) 'The Stages of Life', *Collected Works*, Volume 10.

—— (1931d) 'Mind and Earth', *Collected Works*, Volume 10.

—— (1931e) 'Archaic Man', *Collected Works*, Volume 10.

—— (1931f) 'The Aims of Psychotherapy', *Collected Works*, Volume 16.

—— (1931g) 'Introduction to Wickes' *The Inner World of Childhood*', *Collected Works*, Volume 17.

—— (1932) 'On the Tale of the Otter', *Collected Works*, Volume 18.

—— (1933) 'The Real and the Surreal', *Collected Works*, Volume 8.

—— (1934a) 'A Review of the Complex Theory', *Collected Works*, Volume 8.

—— (1934b) 'The State of Psychotherapy Today', *Collected Works*, Volume 10.

—— (1934c) 'The Practical Use of Dream-Analysis', *Collected Works*, Volume 16.

—— (1934d) 'The Development of Personality', *Collected Works*, Volume 17.

—— (1934e) 'A Study in the Process of Individuation', *Collected Works*, Volume 9i.

—— (1935a) 'The Tavistock Lectures', *Collected Works*, Volume 18.

—— (1935b) 'Principles of Practical Psychotherapy', *Collected Works*, Volume 16.

—— (1936a) 'The Concept of the Collective Unconscious', *Collected Works*, Volume 9i.

—— (1936b) 'Psychology and National Problems', *Collected Works*, Volume 18.

—— (1936c) 'Individual Dream Symbolism in Relation to Alchemy', *Collected Works*, Volume 12.

—— (1937) 'The Realities of Practical Psychotherapy', *Collected Works*, Volume 16.

—— (1939a) 'Conscious, Unconscious, and Individuation', *Collected Works*, Volume 9i.

—— (1939b) 'The Symbolic Life', *Collected Works*, Volume 18.

—— (1940) 'The Psychology of the Child Archetype', *Collected Works*, Volume 9i.

—— (1941) 'The Psychological Aspects of the Kore', *Collected Works*, Volume 9i.

—— (1943a) 'Psychotherapy and a Philosophy of Life', *Collected Works*, Volume 16.

—— (1943b) 'Depth Psychology and Self-Knowledge', *Collected Works*, Volume 18.

—— (1944) *Psychology and Alchemy*, *Collected Works*, Volume 12.

—— (1945) 'Medicine and Psychotherapy', *Collected Works*, Volume 16.

—— (1946) 'The Psychology of the Transference', *Collected Works*, Volume 16.

—— (1948a) 'General Aspects of Dream Psychology', *Collected Works*, Volume 8.

—— (1948b) 'Depth Psychology', *Collected Works*, Volume 18.

—— (1948c) 'Techniques of Attitude Change Conducive to World Peace', *Collected Works*, Volume 18.

—— (1949a) 'Foreword to Harding: *Women's Mysteries*', *Collected Works*, Volume 18.

—— (1949b) 'Foreword to Neumann: *Depth Psychology and a New Ethic*', *Collected Works*, Volume 18.

—— (1950a) 'A Study in the Process of Individuation', *Collected Works*, Volume 9i.

—— (1950b) 'Concerning Mandala Symbolism', *Collected Works*, Volume 9i.

—— (1951a) *Aion*, *Collected Works*, Volume 9ii.

—— (1951b) 'Fundamental Questions of Psychotherapy', *Collected Works*, Volume 16.

—— (1952a) 'Synchronicity: An Acausal Connecting Principle', *Collected Works*, Volume 8.

—— (1952b) 'Religion and Psychology: A Reply to Martin Buber', *Collected Works*, Volume 18.

—— (1953a) 'Psychological Commentary on *The Tibetan Book of the Dead*', *Collected Works*, Volume 11.

—— (1953b) 'Foreword to Perry: *The Self in Psychotic Process*', *Collected Works*, Volume 18.

—— (1954a) 'On the Nature of the Psyche', *Collected Works*, Volume 8.

—— (1954b) 'Archetypes of the Collective Unconscious', *Collected Works*, Volume 9i.

—— (1954c) 'Concerning the Archetypes, with Special Reference to the Anima Concept', *Collected Works*, Volume 9i.

—— (1954d) 'Psychological Aspects of the Mother Archetype', *Collected Works*, Volume 9i.

—— (1955–6) *Mysterium Coniunctionis*, *Collected Works*, Volume 14.

—— (1957) 'The Undiscovered Self', *Collected Works*, Volume 10.

—— (1958a) 'Schizophrenia', *Collected Works*, Volume 3.

—— (1958b) 'Flying Saucers: A Modern Myth', *Collected Works*, Volume 10.

—— (1958c) 'Foreword to the Swiss Edition', *Collected Works*, Volume 16.

—— (1958d) 'Jung and Religious Belief', *Collected Works*, Volume 18.

—— (1961a) 'Symbols and the Interpretation of Dreams', *Collected Works*, Volume 18.

—— (1961b) *Memories, Dreams, Reflections*, recorded and edited by Aniela Jaffe, New York: Vintage Books.

—— (1973a) *Psychological Reflections*, J. Jacobi and R.F.C. Hull (eds), Princeton: Princeton University Press.

—— (1973b) *Letters*, Vol. 1, G. Adler (ed.), Princeton: Princeton University Press.

—— (1973c) *Letters*, Vol. 2, G. Adler (ed.), Princeton: Princeton University Press.

—— (1976) *The Visions Seminar*, 2 vols, Zurich: Spring Publications.

Knight, R. (1965) 'Preface' to *Collected Papers on Schizophrenia and Related Subjects* by H.F. Searles, New York: International Universities Press.

Kohut, H. (1971) *The Analysis of the Self*, New York: International Universities Press.

—— (1977) *The Restoration of the Self*, New York: International Universities Press.

Kugler, P. and Hillman, J. (1985) 'The Autonomous Psyche: A Communication to Goodheart from the Bi-personal Field of Paul Kugler and James Hillman', *Spring*, 1985: 141–85.

Laing, R.D. (1965) *The Divided Self*, London: Penguin Books.

—— (1967) *The Politics of Experience*, New York: Ballantine.

Langs, R. (1978) *Technique in Transition*, New York: Aronson.

Langs, R. and Searles, H.F. (1980) *Intrapsychic and Interpersonal Dimensions of Treatment: A Clinical Dialogue*, New York: Aronson.

McGuire, W. and Hull, R.F.C. (eds) (1977) *C.G. Jung Speaking*, Princeton: Princeton University Press.

Maddi, S. (1980) *Personality Theories*, 3rd edn, Homewood: Dorsey.

Masterson, J. (1985) *The Real Self*, New York: Brunner/Mazel.

Mattoon, M.A. (1981) *Jungian Psychology in Perspective*, New York: Free Press.

May, R. (ed.) (1961) *Existential Psychology*, New York: Random House.

Mindell, A. (1975) 'The Golem', *Quadrant*, 8: 108–14.

Minuchin, S. (1974) *Families and Family Therapy*, Cambridge: Harvard University Press.

Misiak, H. and Sexton, V. (1966) *History of Psychology: An Overview*, New York: Grune and Stratton.

Mowrer, O. (1960) 'Sin – The Lesser of Two Evils', *American Psychologist*, 15: 301–4.

Murphy, G. and Kovach, J. (1972) *An Historical Introduction to Modern Psychology*, 3rd edn, New York: Harcourt, Brace and World.

Parks, S. (1987) 'Experiments in Appropriating a New Way of Listening', *Journal of Analytical Psychology*, 32: 93–115.

Peters, R. (ed.) (1962) *Brett's History of Psychology*, New York: Macmillan.

Plaut, A. (1956) 'The Transference in Analytical Psychology', *Technique in Jungian Analysis*, M. Fordham *et al.* (eds), London: Heinemann.

Roazen, P. (1976) *Freud and his Followers*, New York: New American Library.

Samuels, A. (1985) *Jung and the Post-Jungians*, London: Routledge and Kegan Paul.

—— (1989) *The Plural Psyche*, London: Routledge.

Sandler, J., Dare, C. and Holder, A. (1972) 'Frames of Reference in Psychoanalytic Psychology: II. The Historical Context and Phases in the Development of Psychoanalysis', *British Journal of Medical Psychology*, 45: 133–42.

Satinover, J. (1984) 'Jung's Lost Contribution to the Dilemma of Narcissism', *Journal of the American Psychoanalytic Association*, 34: 401–38.

—— (1985) 'At the Mercy of Another: Abandonment and Restitution in Psychosis and Psychotic Character', *Chiron*, 1985: 47–86.

Schultz, D. (1969) *A History of Modern Psychology*, New York: Academic Press.

Schwartz-Salant, N. (1986) 'On the Subtle Body Concept in Clinical Practice', *Chiron*, 1986: 19–58.

—— (1988a) 'Before the Creation: The Unconscious Couple in Borderline States of Mind', *Chiron*, 1988: 1–40.

—— (1988b) 'Archetypal Foundations of Projective Identification', *Journal of Analytical Psychology*, 33: 39–59.

Searles, H.F. (1949/79) 'Concerning Transference and Countertransference', *International Journal of Psychoanalytic Psychotherapy*, 7: 165–88.

—— (1951) 'Data Concerning Certain Manifestations of Incorporation', *Collected Papers on Schizophrenia and Related Subjects*, New York: International Universities Press, 1965. [This book will hereafter be referred to as *Collected Papers on Schizophrenia*.]

—— (1952) 'Concerning a Psychodynamic Function of Perplexity, Confusion, Suspicion and Related Mental States', *Collected Papers on Schizophrenia*.

—— (1955a) 'Dependency Processes in Schizophrenia', *Collected Papers on Schizophrenia*.

—— (1955b) 'The Informational Value of the Supervisor's Emotional Experiences', *Collected Papers on Schizophrenia*.

—— (1956) 'The Psychodynamics of Vengefulness', *Collected Papers on Schizophrenia*.

—— (1958a) 'The Schizophrenic's Vulnerability to the Therapist's Unconscious Processes', *Collected Papers on Schizophrenia*.

—— (1958b) 'Positive Feelings in the Relationship between the Schizophrenic and His Mother', *Collected Papers on Schizophrenia*.

—— (1959a) 'The Effort to Drive the Other Person Crazy – An Element in the Aetiology and Psychotherapy of Schizophrenia', *Collected Papers on Schizophrenia*.

—— (1959b) 'Oedipal Love in the Countertransference', *Collected Papers on Schizophrenia*.

—— (1959c) 'Integration and Differentiation in Schizophrenia', *Collected Papers on Schizophrenia*.

—— (1959d) 'Integration and Differentiation in Schizophrenia: An Over-All View', *Collected Papers on Schizophrenia*.

—— (1960) *The Nonhuman Environment*, New York: International Universities Press.

—— (1961a) 'The Evolution of the Mother Transference in Psychotherapy with the Schizophrenic Patient', *Collected Papers on Schizophrenia*.

—— (1961b) 'Schizophrenic Communication', *Collected Papers on Schizophrenia*.

—— (1961c) 'Sexual Processes in Schizophrenia', *Collected Papers on Schizophrenia*.

—— (1961d) 'Anxiety Concerning Change, as Seen in the Psychotherapy of Schizophrenic Patients – with Particular Reference to the Sense of Personal Identity', *Collected Papers on Schizophrenia*.

—— (1961e) 'The Sources of Anxiety in Paranoid Schizophrenia', *Collected Papers on Schizophrenia*.

—— (1961f) 'Schizophrenia and the Inevitability of Death', *Collected Papers on Schizophrenia*.

—— (1961g) 'Phases of Patient–Therapist Interaction in the Psychotherapy of Chronic Schizophrenia', *Collected Papers on Schizophrenia*.

—— (1962a) 'The Differentiation Between Concrete and Metaphorical Thinking in the Recovering Schizophrenic Patient', *Collected Papers on Schizophrenia.*

—— (1962b) 'Problems of Psycho-Analytic Supervision', *Collected Papers on Schizophrenia.*

—— (1962c) 'Scorn, Disillusionment, and Adoration in the Psychotherapy of Schizophrenia', *Collected Papers on Schizophrenia.*

—— (1963a) 'The Place of Neutral Therapist-Responses in Psychotherapy with the Schizophrenic Patient', *Collected Papers on Schizophrenia.*

—— (1963b) 'Transference Psychosis in the Psychotherapy of Schizophrenia', *Collected Papers on Schizophrenia.*

—— (1964) 'The Contributions of Family Treatment to the Psychotherapy of Schizophrenia', *Collected Papers on Schizophrenia.*

—— (1965a) *Collected Papers on Schizophrenia*, New York: International Universities Press.

—— (1965b) 'Author's Introduction', *Collected Papers on Schizophrenia.*

—— (1966a) 'Feelings of Guilt in the Psychoanalyst', *Countertransference and Related Subjects*, New York: International Universities Press, 1979. [This book will hereafter be referred to as *Countertransference.*]

—— (1966b) 'Identity Development in Edith Jacobson's *The Self and the Object World'*, *Countertransference.*

—— (1966–7) 'Concerning the Development of an Identity', *Countertransference.*

—— (1967a) 'The Schizophrenic Individual's Experience of his World', *Countertransference.*

—— (1967b) 'The "Dedicated Physician" in the Field of Psychotherapy and Psychoanalysis', *Countertransference.*

—— (1968) 'Paranoid Processes Among Members of the Therapeutic Team', *Countertransference.*

—— (1969) 'A Case of Borderline Thought Disorder', *Countertransference.*

—— (1970a) 'Autism and the Phase of Transition to Therapeutic Symbiosis', *Countertransference.*

—— (1970b) 'An Epic Struggle with Schizophrenia: A Review of Marion Milner's *The Hands of the Living God'*, *Countertransference.*

—— (1971) 'Pathologic Symbiosis and Autism', *Countertransference.*

—— (1972a) 'The Function of the Patient's Realistic Perceptions of the Analyst in Delusional Transference', *Countertransference.*

—— (1972b) 'Unconscious Processes in Relation to the Environmental Crisis', *Countertransference.*

—— (1972c) 'Intensive Psychotherapy of Chronic Schizophrenia: A Case Report', *Countertransference.*

—— (1973a) 'Concerning Therapeutic Symbiosis: The Patient as Symbiotic Therapist, the Phase of Ambivalent Symbiosis, and the Role of Jealousy in the Fragmented Ego', *Countertransference.*

—— (1973b) 'Some Aspects of Unconscious Fantasy', *Countertransference.*

—— (1973c) 'Violence in Schizophrenia', *Countertransference.*

—— (1975a) 'The Patient as Therapist to his Analyst', *Countertransference.*

—— (1975b) 'Countertransference and Theoretical Model', *Countertransference.*

—— (1976a) 'Transitional Phenomena and Therapeutic Symbiosis', *Countertransference*.

—— (1976b) 'Psychoanalytic Therapy with Schizophrenic Patients in a Private-Practice Context', *Countertransference*.

—— (1976c) 'The Countertransference in the Borderline Patient', in J. Leboit and A. Caponi (eds) *Advances in the Psychotherapy of the Borderline Patient*, New York: Aronson, 1979.

—— (1976d) 'Jealousy Involving an Internal Object', in J. Leboit and A. Caponi (eds) *Advances in the Psychotherapy of the Borderline Patient*, New York: Aronson, 1979.

—— (1977a) 'Dual- and Multiple-Identity Processes in Borderline Ego Functioning', *Countertransference*.

—— (1977b) 'The Development of Mature Hope in the Patient–Therapist Relationship', *Countertransference*.

—— (1977c) 'The Analyst's Participant Observation as Influenced by the Patient's Transference', *Countertransference*.

—— (1977d) 'Discussion of "The Concept of Psychoses as a Result and in the Context of the Long-Term Treatment Modalities," by Leopold Bellak', *Countertransference*.

—— (1978) 'Psychoanalytic Therapy with the Borderline Adult: Some Principles Concerning Technique', in J. Masterson (ed.) *New Perspectives on the Psychotherapy of the Borderline Adult*, New York: Brunner/Mazel.

—— (1979) *Countertransference and Related Subjects*, New York: International Universities Press.

—— (1980) [See Searles and Langs (1980).]

—— (1984) 'The Role of the Analyst's Facial Expressions in Psychoanalysis and Psychoanalytic Psychotherapy', *My Work With Borderline Patients*, New York: Aronson [1986].

—— (1986) *My Work With Borderline Patients*, New York: Aronson.

Searles, H.F. and Langs, R. (1980) *Intrapsychic and Interpersonal Dimensions of Treatment*, New York: Aronson.

Sechehaye, M. (1951) *Symbolic Realization*, New York: International Universities Press.

Sedgwick, D. (1983) *Towards a further Integration of Analytical Psychology with other Forms of Psychotherapy: C.G. Jung and Harold Searles Compared* (Unpublished Doctoral Thesis) [*Dissertation Abstracts International*: 44/09A, Publication No. : AAC8400930].

Selesnick, S. (1963) 'C.G. Jung's Contribution to Psychoanalysis', *American Journal of Psychiatry*, 120: 350–6.

Smith, M., Glass, G. and Miller, T. (1981) *The Benefits of Psychotherapy*, Baltimore: Johns Hopkins University Press.

Strupp, H. (1973) *Psychotherapy: Clinical, Research and Theoretical Issues*, New York: Aronson.

Sullivan, B. (1987) 'The Archetypal Foundation of the Therapeutic Process', *Chiron*, 1987: 27–50.

—— (1989) *Psychotherapy Grounded in the Feminine Principle*, Willmette: Chiron Publications.

Sullivan, H. (1940) *Conceptions of Modern Psychiatry*, New York: Norton, 1953.

Schwartz-Salant, N. (1982) *Narcissism and Character Transformation*, Toronto: Inner City Books.

Szasz, T. (1960) 'The Myth of Mental Illness', *American Psychologist*, 15: 113–18.

Tansey, M. and Burke, W. (1987) *Understanding Countertransference: From Projective Identification to Empathy*, Hillsdale: Analytic Press.

Tower, L. (1956) 'Countertransference', *Journal of the American Psychoanalytic Association*, 4: 224–55.

Ulanov, A. (1982) 'How Do I Assess Progress in Supervision?', *Journal of Analytical Psychology*, 27: 122–6.

Watson, R. (1968) *The Great Psychologists*, Philadelphia: Lippincott.

Weigert, E. (1952) 'Contribution to the Problem of Termination in Psychoanalysis', *Psychoanalytic Quarterly*, 21: 465–80.

—— (1954) 'Countertransference and Self-Analysis of the Psychoanalyst', *International Journal of Psychoanalysis*, 35: 242–6.

Whitaker, C. and Keith, D. (1981) 'Symbolic-Experiential Family Therapy', in A. Gurman and D. Kniskern (eds) *Handbook of Family Therapy*, New York: Brunner/Mazel.

Winnicott, D. (1964) 'Review of C.G. Jung's "Memories, Dreams, Reflections" ', *International Journal of Psychoanalysis*, 45: 450–5.

—— (1968) 'The Use of an Object and Relating Through Identifications', *Playing and Reality*, London: Tavistock, 1971.

Young-Eisendrath, P. (1984) *Hags and Heroes: A Feminist Approach to Jungian Psychotherapy with Couples*, Toronto: Inner City.

Young-Eisendrath, P. and Weidemann, F. (1987) *Female Authority*, New York: Guilford.

Zetzel, E. (1956) 'Current Concepts of Transference', *International Journal of Psychoanalysis*, 37: 369–76.

NAME INDEX

Adler, A. 8
Arlow, J. 5

Bateson, G. 39
Bion, W. 1
Bleuler, E. 8
Brome, V. 22

Coles, R. 7

Dare, C. 5

Ellenberger, H. 2, 22, 121
Ellis, A. 5
Evans, R. 5

Fordham, M. 2, 4, 5, 9
Freud, S. 2, 4, 6, 8, 9, 11, 38, 63
Frey-Rohn, L. 6
Friedman, P. 5
Fromm, E. 4

Gendlin, E. 5
Glass, G. 9, 39, 152, 154
Glover, E. 4
Goldstein, J. 5
Goodheart, W. 1, 7
Guntrip, H. 3

Hall, C. 5
Harms, E. 4
Heimann, P. 2
Henderson, J. 3
Holder, A. 5

Jacobi, J. 4
Jacoby, M. 7

Klein, M. 1, 8
Knight, R. 7, 87, 150
Kohut, H. 1, 8
Kovach, J. 5

Laing, R. 5, 39
Langs, R. 1, 2, 7, 88
Lindszay, G. 5
Little, M. 2

Maddi, S. 4, 5
Maslow, A. 5
Masterson, J. 5
Mattoon, M. 4
May, R. 39
Miller, T. 9, 39, 152, 154
Minuchin, S. 39
Misiak, H. 4
Mowrer, O. 39
Murphy, G. 5

Perls, F. 5
Peters, R. 4

Racker, H. 1, 2
Rank, O. 8
Roazen, P. 2
Rogers, C. 5

Samuels, A. 2, 4
Sandler, J. 5

SUBJECT INDEX

active imagination 13, 28, 95, 96, 109
affect-ego 13
affectivity 25, 46, 121, 143
albedo 114, 116
alchemy 4, 33, 111, 118, 138, 147
American Psychoanalytic Association 8
ambivalence 17, 27, 31, 48, 50, 54
ambivalent symbiosis *see* symbiosis
amplification 95, 109
analyst *see* therapist
analyst–patient relationship *see* therapist–client relationship, transference
analytic process *see* process of psychotherapy, transference
analytic couch 88
ancestral inheritance 55, 58–60
anima 3, 66, 71, 82, 150
animism 19
animus 66, 71, 150
anthropology 20
anticipated psychosis 96
archetypes 12, 15–17, 19, 21, 26, 30, 36, 50–2, 58–62, 64–7, 71, 72, 81, 89, 101, 109, 111, 117, 126, 130, 142, 145–9, 152, 155; child 33; divine child 33, 35, 113, 116; hero 32–4; mother 17, 35; of Self 30, 73 (*see also* Self); as transcendental 59, 81; wounded healer 142

associations 98, 108
atmosphere: of family 56; psychological 25; of transference 91, 96
autism 54
autism stage 66, 113

Bad Mother 17, 30, 51, 89, 112
borderline personality 7, 9, 45

catharsis stage 111
causality 27, 59, 104
child: archetype 33, 35, 113, 116; development 16, 18–21; introjects parents 16, 24; psychotherapeutic striving toward parents 53, 58, 61, 83, 148, 155; -self 55; trauma 96; *see also* individuation, symbiosis
client: as countertransference parent 141; idealizes therapist 134–5; introjected by therapist 78, 80, 82, 130, 140; personality of 81, 93, 117, 133, 134, 140; sadism in 123–4, 127; *see also* psychopathology, therapist
collective unconscious 3, 15, 19, 20, 27–9, 50, 51, 59, 65, 81, 109, 110, 145, 147
complementary identity 114
compensation: in dreams 102, 104; in paranoia 105; in pathology 61; Self as 30

playful loss of ego.

Searles:
1 stage: out of contact;
defense against
therapeutic symbiosis
i.e autism

2. stage therapeutic symbiosis
3. Stage: Individuation

Jung: 1 Separatio: long preliminary
talk

2.) Nigredo: at some point
discussion touches on the
unconscious and establishes
the unconscious identity of
doctor and patient.
(Boundaryless chaos and distrust)

3) Conjunctio (death)
union of opposites in the unconscious
Pregnant with meaning.

④ Purification (divine child, differentiation
symbol of Self / sacrifice

5) Albedo (whitening) consciousness
patient accountable for his
illness